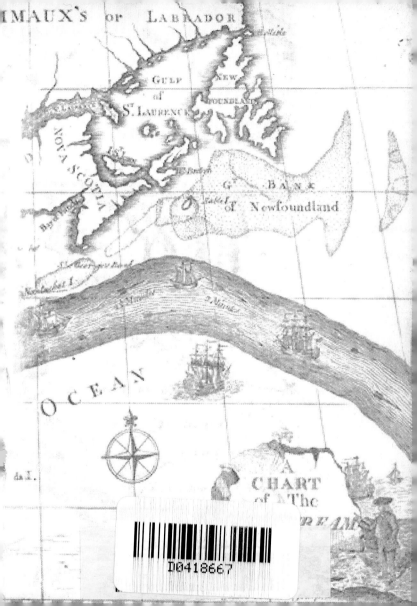

IMAUX'S or LABRADOR

GULF of ST. LAURENCE

NEW FOUNDLAND

NOVA SCOTIA

G. BANK of Newfoundland

OCEAN

A CHART of NThe

Portrait of the
Gulf Stream

Portrait of the Gulf Stream

In praise of currents

by
Érik Orsenna
member of the Académie française

translated from the French by
Moishe Black

HAUS PUBLISHING
London

Copyright © Érik Orsenna

English language translation copyright © Moishe Black

First published in Great Britain in 2008 by Haus Publishing Limited, 26
Cadogan Court, Draycott Avenue, London SW3 3BX
www.hauspublishing.co.uk

Originally published in French by Éditions du Seuil, 2005

The moral rights of the author have been asserted.

A CIP catalogue record for this book is available from the British Library

ISBN 978-1-905791-33-0

Typeset in Garamond 3 by MacGuru Ltd
info@macguru.org.uk
Printed and bound by Graphicom in Vicenza, Italy

This book is supported by the French Ministry of
Foreign Affairs as part of the Burgess programme
run by the Cultural Department of the French Embassy in
London.

For my father

Siéntate, mar,
Que tenemos que hablar
De nuestra vida
Bajo la luz de la fantasía

Rafael Alberti

"Sit you down, o sea,
For we have to talk
About our life
In the light of fantasy."

Contents

Before We Embark

I am not a scientist, I am a wanderer. A wanderer with a special weakness for the sort of trivial questions that leave not only parents but even experts fumbling around for an answer: Why is the night dark? Why does water wet? ... And why do currents flow?

It so happens that ever since childhood I have been in love with ocean currents, in love with those rivers hidden in the water. I love letting a current catch me up, and then drifting, as though I were on holiday: someone strong has suddenly taken you into the palm of his hand. All you have to do now is let yourself be carried along.

But equally do I love to work my way upstream, tacking for hours in a sailboat, making headway yard by yard, and who cares if darkness falls, and as for resorting to the motor, not a chance! The matador does not work his bull with a submachine gun. I love those little friends you didn't know were there, who will gladly lend a hand on such occasions: I mean the counter-currents. They come in light shapes, loops, swirls. Everything about them is troll-like, elfin. They call out to you and you wonder: should I answer? Is their kind offer some sort of trap? After all, they only live in coastal waters, near the shore, too near. Won't I "go aground," "strike bottom," in other words hit a rock or even wreck my boat if I come too close?

I enjoy looking at navigators' charts, the kind that are covered with black arrows of every size, pointing in every direction. These charts set themselves an impossible task, that of defining the indefinable, of mapping out the unpredictable behavior of ocean currents from one hour to the next.

I can imagine someone making comparable maps for our so-called *terra firma*. It is a well established fact that Earth's land mass is perturbed by forces that are unbelievably ill-charted. We know that lava flows, of course, but that is not the whole story. Everywhere beneath our feet, things are constantly on the move, sliding, forming hollows, collapsing. Not to mention those great, big, heavy continents. Stout though they may be, it would appear that they are drifting. Geography itself is a kind of navigation.

As for our bodies, our own bodies, China settled that question thousands of years ago. With the invention of acupuncture, the Chinese proved that it all comes down to energy. To treat the body, you merely have to ascertain the channels along which energy travels and prick the spots where it accumulates. To put it simply, it's a matter of currents.

I remember the day that my father taught me about drift. The same father who, for years and years, told me stories about a tugboat to help me fall asleep. I must have been seven or eight years old. We were out for a boatride. Without any warning he handed the tiller over to me. "All right, now, take her back into the bay." I made straight for a point midway between the twin buoys, the green one and the red. And of course I missed the channel: our dear old Kerpont current had carried us onto the rocks, a good quarter of a mile to the north. The reader will understand why I have distrusted straight lines ever since.

Upon careful reflection, I would say that my dealings with currents have taught me self-reliance, obstinacy and cunning. It was time for me to acknowledge this generosity.

⌒

As others do with stamps or butterflies, so I collect currents, taking advantage of each nautical journey to add to the list, but in my collection the Gulf Stream holds undisputed pride of place.

In my family, Catholic by tradition, it was understood that some of our prayers should express gratitude to God (for all His works) and, a close second, gratitude to the Gulf Stream. Every time we emerged shaking and shivering from our icy Breton swims, a grandmother or an aunt would be there to exclaim: "Now don't forget to thank the Gulf Stream! If not for the Gulf Stream, our ocean would be cold." And every stroll around the garden included its share of praises. "How well that palm tree is doing; it reminds me of Algiers! Look how high that century-plant has grown; anyone would think this was Madagascar. Truly, the Gulf Stream has showered us with gifts again this year."

What the Gulf Stream actually did was to console us for the loss of our colonies. With its gifts of warm water and mild air, it had allowed us to bring home to the mother country the best features of our late empire. The English passion for rhododendrons, as I shall attempt to show, springs from very similar nostalgic sources.

↩

The Gulf Stream has never left me.

But our relationship has changed gradually over time.

Uneasiness and doubt have taken the place of my continuing obligation to feel gratitude.

The uneasiness, shared by increasing numbers of

people, has to do with the health, indeed the survival of my beloved Gulf Stream. The unease is all the more disturbing for being based on a paradox: is global warming going to kill this current of warm water?

Specialists are bitterly divided on the matter. And their debate leads to a fundamental questioning that to me is an even greater torment than the uncertainty I just mentioned; it involves doubt. What if the Gulf Stream is a sham? What if its title of Great Benefactor is nothing but a false claim? To put it in a nutshell, are we in fact indebted to the Gulf Stream for the extremely temperate climate we enjoy here in old Europe?

This hypothesis, as I'm sure you realize, threatens to topple one of the pillars of my existence, one of the few axioms on which I could always count for support.

For a long time, I have chosen to avoid the issue.

But the day has come. I must now take my courage in my hands and sally forth, along byways and seaways, to meet the experts and see the places for myself.

I

A Short Introduction to General Motion

" … an oscillation inside the earth … "
Plato, *Phaedo*

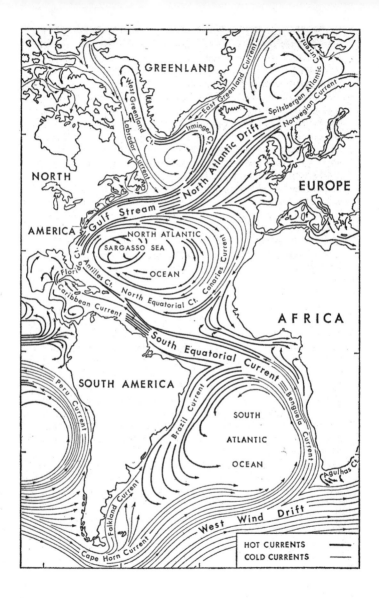

1

Why the Sea Moves

The sea "exists": you can touch it. At the same time, water has no inherent shape; that is to say, it can assume any given shape.

This dual nature of the sea, at once material and formless, explains why so many cosmogonies place an ocean at the origin of origins. From out of the sea comes life. Then begins the adventure of diversity.

It should be pointed out that science offers essentially the same explanation.

⤿

Jacques Lacarrière has not confined himself to exploring the Greek summer (*L'Été grec*). From his journey to the heart of mythologies (*Au Coeur des mythologies*), he returns bearing treasures.

This is how a certain Ibn Abbas, interpreting an Arab tradition, describes the birth of the world: "God created a white pearl whose dimensions were those of the earth and sky. The pearl has seven thousand tongues, each of them glorifying God in seven thousand languages ... . *Then God called upon {the white pearl}. The pearl shuddered at his summons, shuddered so hard that it turned into flowing, moving water. All things now suspend for a time their praises unto the Creator, save only water which endlessly glorifies him with its trembling and its turbulence.* That is why God elected water, in preference over other created things, to be the origin of them all. Then an order was given that water should cease its restless stirring, and so it stopped and waited for a sign from God."

2

Volcanic Tides

From time immemorial, the little moon Io has revolved around Jupiter the huge. How could the smaller body fail to be attracted by the pull of the greater? Jupiter's force of attraction triggers uncontrollable tides on Io.

But they are rather special tides, for there is no water on Io, hence no ocean.

The tides on Io are tides of lava. They are volcanic eruptions, magnetic ebb-tides and seismic flood-tides.

Whether they be on Io or here on Earth, composed of lava or of water, tides are the net result of a veritable host of mobile tendencies acting one upon the other. Our planet, for instance, which we think of as perfectly round, is constantly changing its shape. Every twelve hours its surface rises and falls by several tenths of a meter. Isaac Newton had predicted this mobility. Much later, the English mathematician Love gave his name to a number expressing the deformation of Earth in response to the attractive force of the Moon and the Sun.

3

The Moon is Moving Further Away

Over the past thirty-five years, astronauts have set up on the surface of the moon all sorts of instruments, including reflecting panels. The panels represent a domain in which France pioneered as early as the 1960s. The basic unit is a box, with a lid that opens after the clouds of dust raised by the moon landing have had time to settle. Looking inside the box, your first reaction is that it contains precious stones. In fact, there is just an irregular glass surface studded with corners and pointed tips. Earth stations – one of them is in Grasse, high up above the fields of flowers – emit a laser beam at these panels. When the beam arrives, it is reflected in their glass surfaces before returning to its point of departure. Once the amount of time required for this journey has been established, it is possible to calculate the distance from the Earth to the Moon with an accuracy in the order of one centimeter.

That distance is not constant. It varies in relation to a number of factors. On average, we are separated from our satellite by 400,000 kilometers. But the return trips of the laser beam have also brought us another piece of news, this one rather sad: the Moon is leaving us. It is moving away. Moving away slowly but surely: each year, the space between us increases by 3.8 centimeters.

If we cannot prevent this phenomenon of growing apart, can we at least explain it?

When a married couple fall upon unhappy times, there is always responsibility on both sides. I do not propose, in these pages, to delve into so painful a subject. Such an inquiry would bring to light the influence of those immense waves contained within the oceans' inner workings, fierce struggles between powerful sources of energy, vast processes of compensation …

The fact remains.

8

earth's gravity decreasing

4

Continents and Sea Bottoms: Global Drift

M arburg is a small city in the heart of Germany: to the west is Cologne, to the south Frankfurt. Imagine a fine day in 1910; a professor at the local university is skimming through an article in the library when suddenly he gives a start of surprise. The author of the article states categorically that the plants and animals found in a fossilized state on the two shores of the Atlantic are alike.

How can such extreme similarity be explained? Could bridges, now collapsed, once have existed between the two continents?

Suddenly a different hypothesis presents itself to the professor's mind. It should be noted that he habitually deals with things that move. He is an astronomer by training, and his hobby is flying in hot-air balloons. For a while, he and his brother held the world record for this type of flight (52 hours and 30 minutes). But his real specialty is meteorology. His work in that field has several times led him to set off for Greenland, where he can study the circulation of polar air.

His idea is a simple one: the continents have moved. Close scrutiny of the two coastlines and their shape inevitably strengthens him in his conviction. Bring Africa close to America and they fit together. Mauritania nestles unprotestingly into the Gulf of Mexico. Lisbon becomes a suburb of New York; Caracas merges with Lagos; Brazil and Angola are now one entity.

Outbreak of the Great War. The professor is mobilized for military service. Wounded early in the conflict, he is able to resume his scholarly work. And in 1915 there appears *The Origin of Continents and Oceans*. Alfred Lothar Wegener has just revolutionized the history of the Earth.

↬

Two hundred and seventy million years ago, there existed a single continent, Pangaea. Little by little, it broke up, giving birth to five pieces, our five continents. The process did not stop there. The five continents went their separate ways. They moved along like ships. At their prow, there was a crumpling effect: so the mountains sprang up. At their stern, they shed chunks of themselves along their course: so strings of islands were born.

You can imagine the outcry. Scientists, as well as people of "ordinary common sense" were up in arms: What crazy notion is this? If *terra firma* moves, what are we left with that can be called permanent? And besides, if the continents are nomadic, as this person is claiming, what makes them move? Professor Wegener's arguments are not very convincing. He speaks of "centrifugal forces," or the influence of the tides ...

Twenty-five years went by in largely unproductive debate.

↜

Harry Hammond Hess was a professor of geology at Princeton University. The Second World War would change his life ... and impart fresh momentum to earth sciences. Hess enlisted in the navy and was soon given command of a ship. What does a scientist do aboard a seagoing vessel? When military tasks do not require all his attention, he does research. He takes samples, he takes measurements, he takes time to reflect. Why are the rocks that have emerged from the ocean depths so *young*? Are we to infer that the ocean floor is continuously renewing itself? Harry Hess has an explanation to offer.

How did the single continent break up? For anyone who wants to have some notion of this matter, the best possible approach today is a tour of East Africa. The *Great Rift*, which goes from Ethiopia to South Africa, is a depression resulting from a cave-in, a broad valley dotted with lakes whose waters are slowly evaporating. The earth's crust here is becoming thinner and thinner. A volcano is thrusting its way up through the crust. To be followed by many others. Soon, the sea will invade the Rift.

That is how the single continent broke up.

Since then, each of the fragments has lived its own life.

Some are moving away from each other, for instance America from Europe (two centimeters a year). Others are drawing closer to one another, for instance Africa to Europe (same rate of progress).

Did you think the ocean floor was fixed and motionless? Wrong. Chains of undersea volcanos are unremittingly active down there. From their flows of lava, *plates* are born, those plates on which the continents rest ...

⤚

Such, but stripped down to its bare essentials, is the epic tale unfolded for me by Claude Allègre. It was, I remember, a winter's day in Paris, on the place de l'Odéon, opposite the theatre of that name, a long way from any volcano so far discovered. I remember how as he spoke, I was thinking: "What a fool I've been to neglect science all these years; natural history

13

is the mother of every form of history, every sort of story, the novel of all novels."

Allègre had taken out a pen and shoved the glass to one side, and he was now cursing the tablecloth for not being one of those old disposable paper ones. But a moment later he changed his mind. After all, words should be enough; no need for diagrams.

༄

Exactly one year later, on Sunday, 26 December 2004, the Indo-Australian oceanic plate was passing under the Burmese microplate, with the result we all know: a terrible tsunami and 250,000 deaths.

5

The Relieving of Norway

At the beginning of the last century, certain Norwegian scientists began to wonder. They looked thoughtfully at the dark line on the rocks along the coast, marking the highest point reached by sea waters in days gone by.

Then they compared this line with the high-water marks of their own era.

"It really does seem as though the level of the sea is going down."

How could they ever have suspected the truth? It was the land, their land, that was going up.

During periods of extreme cold, and especially 20,000 years ago, Norway was gradually covered with a coat of ice that in some places may have reached a thickness of more than 2,000 meters. The country sank under the weight of ice.[1]

When the weather became milder, those layers of ice began to melt and slide away.

Gradually Norway rid itself of its heavy, heavy mantle.

Relieved, the country stretched and rose up.

Rose up like a raft that has been discharged of its load.

And the upward movement has continued ever since. Each year, Norway progresses skyward by a good centimeter.

To this upward progression scientists give the charming name 'post-glacial rebound.'

6

Gaspard Gustave Coriolis (1792–1843)

The year is 1780. Following in Lafayette's footsteps, Rochambeau arrives in America with an army. He brings the official support of King Louis XVI for the *insurgents* fighting against the British crown. Among his officers is one Jean-Baptiste Elzéar Coriolis, who will not long remain a soldier. Scarcely has he returned to France when the Revolution breaks out. Jean-Baptiste leaves Paris in all haste and moves to the city of Nancy where he becomes a manufacturer. Did he tell the story of his travels to his son Gaspard, a brilliant but sickly child? We shall never know. Gaspard loved science. In 1808 he was accepted into the newly created École Polytechnique; he was the second highest ranked of all the applicants.

Admitted to the professional body of Civil

Engineers, Gaspard turned his back on the sea to busy himself with the construction of roads and bridges in the Vosges, more particularly in the Département of Meurthe-et-Moselle. But very soon, worn out by that mountainous terrain, he went back to teach in Paris, where the École Polytechnique opened its doors to him. He would end his career and his days at that institute in his capacity as a research supervisor.

Our Gaspard developed a passion for billiards, and even devoted a book to the subject. It was called *Théorie mathématique des effets du jeu de billard*, 'Mathematical theory of effects in the game of billiards', and was perhaps the only piece of writing he ever did just for pleasure: the rest of his life was entirely taken up by unrelenting work. Reared in close proximity to his father's factories, he always sought practical applications for his theoretical research. This led him to explore the most varied fields of inquiry: friction, hydraulics, ergonomics, kinetic energy, the basic concept of work …

But he achieved fame through a book with an austere title: *Sur les équations du mouvement relatif des systèmes de corps*, 'On the equations governing the relative movement of systems of bodies' (1835).

History is often very unfair. Before Coriolis, Laplace had set down equations that were almost identical, but without drawing all the conclusions they implied. And yet the aforesaid Monsieur Laplace knew the sea, knew it very well indeed: to him we owe the first general theory of tides. Humboldt, with no equations but simply from seafaring, had intuitively arrived at the truth. Nor is there any indication that our Gaspard Gustave ever set foot on a boat or ever showed the least interest in the sea. That does not alter the fact: now and for all time, Coriolis is the person who explained the influence of Earth's rotation on the course of winds and currents.

∽

All movement on our planet results from five forces:

- the pressure or driving force;
- the various frictions resisting that force;

- centrifugal force;
- the force of gravity;
- and Coriolis's force.

We have almost no difficulty imagining the first four. The fifth, Coriolis's force, is more abstruse. No one can easily visualize the influence of the Earth's rotation.

As I do not wish to spoil the first phase of our journey, I shall spare you the relevant mathematical statements. Suffice it to say that they explain the course followed by those precious fluids of ours, air and water. Thus, in the Northern Hemisphere, the *winds* and *ocean currents* will always deviate toward the right. In the Southern Hemisphere they will always bear to the left. You should also know that Coriolis's force is zero at the equator, increases with the degree of latitude, and reaches its maximum at the poles.

You now know enough to see your way clearly into a certain number of mysteries, including the *direction* in which currents circulate. Coriolis's force is what makes the Gulf Stream (Atlantic) and the Kuroshio or Japan Current (Pacific) flow along the coasts of America and Asia in a *north-easterly* direction; and it is also the driving force that makes the Atlantic's Brazil Current and the Indian Ocean's Agulhas Current flow down toward the *south*. Note that *kuroshio* means "dark current" in Japanese.

And that is why the Gulf Stream leaves the Gulf of Mexico by the north passage (the Straits of Florida) and not by the southern route (the Venezuelan coast).

7

What Socrates Thought

In the *Phaedo*, Plato describes Socrates's final hours. Before drinking the hemlock, Socrates elaborates his ideas on the destiny of the soul after death. And in the course of his exposition, he comes to discuss rivers, currents and great winds.

> 'In the earth itself [are] monstrous
> unceasing subterranean rivers of waters
> both hot and cold [...]. By these the
> several regions are filled in turn as the
> flood reaches them.
>
> All this movement to and fro is caused
> by an oscillation inside the earth, and this
> oscillation is brought about by natural
> means, as follows.

One of the cavities in the earth is not only larger than the rest, but pierces right through from one side to the other. [...] Into this gulf all the rivers flow together, and from it they flow forth again, and each acquires the nature of that part of the earth through which it flows. The cause of the flowing in and out of all these streams is that the mass of liquid has no bottom or foundation; so it oscillates and surges to and fro, and the air or breath that belongs to it does the same [...]. And just as when we breathe we exhale and inhale the breath in a continuous stream, so in this case too the breath, oscillating with the liquid, causes terrible and monstrous winds as it passes in and out.'[2]

The Relationship of Wind and Sea (continued)

For centuries, those navigators bold enough to venture into the Far North were baffled. Why do icebergs not move in the direction of the wind that is propelling them, but always at an angle of forty-five degrees *to the right?*

In 1902, Swedish oceanographer Vagn Walfrid Ekman came up with the answer. The factor responsible for the strange course steered by icebergs is Coriolis's force.

Ekman goes further. "He shows that the wind, by a process of friction, sets in motion a layer of water about a hundred meters deep. This layer exerts a pull on the layer below that, which in turn deviates to the right. And so on. A spiral develops. The greater the depth, the further a current will deviate to the right.

On average, wind drives the sea at right angles to the direction the wind is blowing. This displacing of water sets off the dance of the gyres, the great whirlpools."

II
Anatomy of a Loop

The river is within us, the sea is all about us.
T.S. Eliot

1

Once Upon a Time there was Benjamin Franklin

The existence of a powerful current, to be encountered as you approached the New World, was known to sailors as early as the 16th century. Juan Ponce de Léon, who accompanied Columbus on his second voyage, had set sail with one special goal in mind: he wanted to find the fountain of youth, the fountain that could assuage forever the dread that torments aging men, the *enflaquecimento del sexo*. That is how he came to discover Florida. In 1513, he had noticed that as soon as he neared the coast, his ship experienced great difficulty making its way southward. And his pilot, Antón de Alaminos, was given the task of establishing the quickest route to Spain.

A century later and a little further north, sailing

close to the Grand Banks of Newfoundland, a certain Marc Lescarbot had had a strange experience "over which," he wrote in his log-book, "a natural philosopher might well ponder." He and his crew had suddenly found themselves squarely in the middle of a flux of warm water while the surrounding air was still frigid. Three days later, on 21 June 1606, the sea had all at once turned cold again.

Endlessly, ship's captains argued among themselves over this mystery of "the river in the heart of the sea." No systematic record existed, nor even the most tentative explanation. As a consequence, it was open season for the wildest speculations. Thus, James Knosc of Bolduc, an Oxford monk, opined that all the currents of all the seas converge upon the North Pole, where together they disappear into an abyss. Four great islands surround the fearful cascade. A black rock, thirty-three leagues across, stands at the very spot that marks the Pole. Ships caught in this raging tide cannot make their way out again, even with the help of a favorable wind.[3]

Though ridiculed by sailors, this theory would

enjoy a great and lasting success. Another geographer of a fantastical turn of mind would, moreover, augment and complete it in the 17th century: the mass of water swallowed up at the North Pole passes through our planet along the axis of rotation down to the South Pole,[4] whence it spreads once again over the surface of the globe.

Given the growing frequency of travel by sea and the curiosity of those travelling, the Gulf Stream was well aware that it could not hope to keep its secrets for long. All that remained was to find the human being worthy of such a revelation.

My reader may smile to see a current, a blind natural force, thus endowed with a soul, or, to put it in today's language, a communication strategy. And yet!

Who better than Franklin deserved to be the recipient of these confidences?

At the time when matters maritime enter his life, he is fifty years old. He is living in a spanking new city, Philadelphia (whose name, derived from Greek, signifies a high ideal: brotherly love). There he leads, concurrently, innumerable lives: he is at once a printer, publisher (in particular of an almanac, *Poor Richard*, that has the noblest of goals: the instruction and edification of his fellow citizens), renowned expert (on all sorts of subjects, including his special passion, electricity; he exchanges letters with the highest scientific authorities; he already has to his credit a number of fairly significant inventions, including the lightning rod), jurist (the American colonies are beginning to emancipate themselves from the tutelage of London; new institutions are needed; he is consulted about most of them), philanthropist (he organizes public street lighting, he founds hospitals), politician (he is a Representative). In short, Benjamin Franklin is the very incarnation of the Enlightenment (he will even embrace its dates, or nearly so, within his own life span, 1706–1790). He has all the attributes: complete confidence in progress through knowledge; a wellspring of energy, flowing unrestricted across artificial dividing lines and outer limits; boundless and boundaryless activity.

And into this full existence comes the Gulf Stream.

Since 1753, Benjamin Franklin had been his city's Postmaster, no less. A logical extension, when you stop to think about it, of all his other responsibilities. What is the use of producing knowledge if nothing is transmitted? And when you believe in progress as passionately as he did, all news is good news, by definition.

His postal employees were at a loss to respond when faced with the anger of their clients. Why were the boats carrying mail from England to America so much slower than American merchant ships? Why did people have to wait two or three weeks longer for those boats?

In the face of this growing discontent, the matter was referred to the central administration, which at that time still meant London. The Admiralty, for all its imposing manner, was stumped. The Admiralty decided to approach Franklin, who in turn contacted a distant cousin of his. Timothy Folger was not just a cousin, he was a sea captain, and he explained this nautical enigma in a single word: the current. The violent current that runs along the coasts, the current so familiar to whales and those who hunted them, the harpooners from Nantucket.

Often, Folger elaborated, we meet boats belonging to the postal authority, sailing painfully against the flow of the waves. It does no good to inform them of other, faster routes: what British captain would place the slightest confidence in the advice of an American crew?

Commissioned by Franklin, Folger put out to sea once more and plotted the course of the much-discussed ocean river. All for nothing: the postal administration contemptuously brushed these data aside. As everyone knows, there is none so blind as he whose eye is governed by haughty pride. So the precious document was published in France, and nowhere else.

At that same time, the Surveyor General of Florida, William Gerard de Brahm, was doing very similar research. The Enlightenment was at last starting to take an interest in the sea. Franklin's fascination would stay with him for the rest of his life. He crossed the Atlantic three times, in 1775, 1776, and 1785. He was the perfect ambassador. To him fell the task of seeing to it that the voice of newly-born America was heard in Old Europe. That was no excuse for remaining idle during the crossing. He was constantly at work, inventing a variety of research tools, fishing lines, bottles and floats, to collect every possible temperature, both surface and subsurface.

～

We are told that we should never trust the false logic of allegories or the facile poetry of suggestive connections. But all the same ... to find an ambassador who is that interested in ocean currents is enough to lift us out of the usual little minuets of diplomacy! And when it emerges that this Atlantic surveyor is the same fellow who has just invented the lightning rod, that tells us how closely related the sea and the sky must be. Unless we know the sky, we shall always remain in ignorance about the sea.

2

On Beginnings

Where does the Gulf Stream begin? Franklin's and de Brahm's initial reports evade the question: both men show a mysterious stream of water coming from Mexico. It passes through the Straits of Florida between Cuba and the Florida Keys, then moves up northward along the American coast before heading east, at the level of Cape Hatteras, to cross the Atlantic.

It's as though, in the minds of those men, a giant spring of water welled up, somewhere there between Yucatan and Louisiana. A spring of water that, in some people's minds (and this belief has persisted), was no more than a resurgence (or simply a continuation) of the Mississippi River, which owes its name to the Chippeway Indians who lived along its banks. *Mee-zee-see-bee:* father of all waters.

Knowledge has progressed, without poetry having to recede. For the "spring of water" is even more mysterious, the story of the Gulf Stream more immense and more enthralling, than anyone thought.

Major currents are not content merely to flow contentedly along in the oceans. Their movements have much greater scope than that. They come to us from much further away, and from much higher up, too. If we are to have any hope of reaching their point of origin and consequently understanding the course they follow, sailing the sea will not suffice. We must work our way back up the chain of effects and causes.

What I mean is, we must leave the watery surfaces and turn our attention to the sky.

To be brief, once upon a time there was the Sun.

As we know, the Sun shines; it sends out rays of sunlight.

But not every part of Earth receives an equal share of the Sun's rays.

From this inequality comes disturbance.

First the atmosphere is disturbed, and that in turn disturbs the sea.

The equator, struck directly by solar rays, receives the greatest share of energy. The air at the equator is hot and light: its pressure is low. A valley of low pressure girdles our planet.

Higher up to the north, or lower down to the south, the Sun's rays strike our planet obliquely. The energy received from the Sun is not as great. The air is colder, denser: its pressure rises. These high-pressure areas are the anticyclones. In our hemisphere, the anticyclone is located near the Azores. In the South Atlantic, it keeps watch over the memory of Napoleon, above the island of Saint Helena.

And, like mountain waters pouring down from the heights, the air will tend to move down from high-pressure areas toward lower-pressure ones, a tendency that will be impeded by Earth's rotation on its own axis.

But the basic principle remains. And that is the origin of winds: they are produced by differences of pressure in the atmosphere. When the force created by these differences is perfectly offset by Coriolis's force, an equilibrium is established. In the Northern hemisphere, air revolves around the anticyclones (clockwise) before wrapping itself around the depressions in the atmosphere (counter-clockwise).

Thus, over the Atlantic, great winds arise at the anticyclones. They come from the north-east in the Northern hemisphere and from the south-east in the Southern hemisphere, and speed towards the equator. Since the 17th century, these winds, known in English as trade winds, have been called in French *alizés*, from an old French word *alis*, itself a form of the modern *lisse*, smooth, regular, for nothing could be more regular than the strength and direction of those winds.

At the other end of the world, in the Indian Ocean, a variant of the same climatic system divides the calendar of winds into two halves. In January, February and March, they blow from India toward Africa. Later they reverse themselves, shifting to the south-west. This is the *monsoon* régime, from the Arabic word *mausim*, meaning "season, a set time."

These winds are routes. Long before the compass needle or the art of reading the stars, they showed sailors their direction and consequently dictated the organizing of trade.

The trade winds propel westward not just ships but also the water that bears them. This water, when it has crossed the Atlantic, threads its obstacle-strewn way into the string of Caribbean islands, and piles up in the Gulf of Mexico. There the surface of the sea is seventy centimeters higher than on the other side of the ocean, at the foot of the Mauritanian cliffs.

A reservoir of this kind cannot go on filling up indefinitely. When they encounter the barrier constituted by Mexico, the waters turn back east (Straits of Florida) with a force hard to imagine: *twenty-five times the total rate of flow of all the rivers in the world.*

That is our current.

Thus, to the question "Where does the Gulf Stream start?", there can be only one answer: in the Sun.

Or, to lay out a more complete family tree, the Sun is the Gulf Stream's great-grandfather, the Azores anticyclone is its grandfather and the trade winds, the *alizé*, its father. To this family let us add the moon.

The little game of tides that the moon plays with the Sun also has a role in this genealogy.

But birth does not tell the whole story of a life.

3

Cape Hatteras – the Glory and the Crimes

In the same way that a political demonstration grows as more sympathizers come to swell its ranks along the route of the march, the Gulf Stream carries more and more water in its train, becoming steadily larger as it moves along the Florida coast. Thirty-one million cubic meters per second as it passes Miami, eighty-five million at Cape Hatteras, and almost double that a little further out into the open sea.

It's breadth is greater than a hundred kilometers. This is indeed the river of which the legends tell. A blue torrent, stretching away out of sight and capable of turning murderous when the north wind rises up to challenge it.

Perhaps the Gulf Stream would like to pursue its course along the coasts of North America? A kind of barrier prevents it doing so: the icy current coming from Labrador and the Greenland Banks. Waters of different temperatures, hence different densities, are not prone to mix. The warmer must give way to the colder. A point opposite Cape Hatteras in North Carolina is where the Gulf Stream bends in its course and heads in a north-easterly direction, toward the Grand Banks of Newfoundland. Its Atlantic crossing has begun.

✐

Cape Hatteras can almost match Cape Horn for shipwrecks. Between Corola and Cape Lookout, more than a thousand vessels have fallen prey to its many traps: shifting shoals, violent currents, frequent hurricanes.

June 1898. Joshua Slocum tells his tale: "The mast is thrashing the air, wildly, swaying this way and that like a reed," the stay snapped, ... though summer was only days away, the weather had unleashed all its fury, "I am being pelted with hailstones [...], lightning is coming crashing down from the clouds, not in isolated flashes but in almost continuous torrents," the boat keeled over ... The old captain was returning to the fold after three years, two months, two days and 46,000 miles. He was completing the first voyage round the world by a sailing-ship with a one-man crew, and it was here that he was being subjected to his most violent storm.

Cape Hatteras. I went, and shuddered at what I saw.

The ebb tide uncovers countless wrecks. In the space of a few hours, the tip of a mast of the schooner *Laura Barnes* († 1921) reappears; the forecastle of the trawler *Lois Joyce* († 1981) surges up; and so does the funnel of the troop transport *Oriental* († 1862) or the last remains of the *Queen Anne's Revenge*, flagship of Blackbeard the Pirate († 1718), before the sea swallows them again.

And on a foggy day there is the endless passing, first in one direction then in the other, of the Flying Dutchman, the mariner who on leaving port failed to take along equipment for casting anchor. As punishment for this unpardonable fault, he was condemned to go on sailing forever.

4

About Ocean Rivers

There are stories past counting, of rivers flowing through the sea. The most beautiful story, because love is involved, comes to us from Greek mythology.[5]

Alpheus is at once a god and a river. The river's course is in Greece, in the Peloponnese. Like all Earth's rivers, it claims Oceanus as its father, and Tethys as its mother. Alpheus is sad. He is in love with a goddess, Artemis, whose only response to him is total indifference: her sole interest is in hunting.

Alpheus does not lose heart. He follows Artemis everywhere, and has decided to take her by force. One fine day, he thinks he sees his chance. The goddess, surrounded by her nymphs, is bathing. The river draws near. Hastily, Artemis daubs her face with mud. Alpheus passes by without recognizing her ...

Weary of these unending attentions, Artemis flees. Using every precaution to keep her plans secret, she makes her way to Sicily, taking refuge in the middle of Syracuse harbor, on the tiny island of Ortygia. She will finally be left in peace, so she thinks. Only to have Alpheus loom up again. At this point in the story, accounts vary. According to some, the river plunges deep into the sea to join his fair one. According to others, Alpheus has changed loves: someone else has caught his fancy, a maidservant of Artemis, called Arethusa. She, to protect her virtue, has changed herself into a fountain. To no avail: Alpheus mingles his waters with those of the fountain.

⇋

For the Greeks, the sea itself, Oceanus, is a river that flows all over our planet (which is a flat, round cake).

Without our penetrating too far into the infinitely complex, shifting jungle of Greek mythology, it is worth our while to sketch the main lines of this family tree. Oceanus is the older son of Heaven (Uranus) and Earth (Gaea). His younger brother is Cronus. Uranus behaves badly toward Gaea: he is constantly getting her with child. Cronus decides to castrate him. He seeks the aid of Oceanus, who refuses to take part in this act of punishment. Some authors would have it that Cronus, future master of the world, is also Chronos, master of Time. In that case Oceanus's refusal would signify that the Ocean refused to become an accomplice of Time …

◠

Jules Verne's passion for the sea is well known. In July 1868, he took possession of his first boat, the *Saint-Michel*, a small ten-ton yacht. He used the boat as his study. It was on board the *Saint-Michel*, cruising the English Channel or peacefully anchored off some welcoming bit of coast, that he would write the greater part of *Twenty Thousand Leagues Under the Sea*. As he sailed between Le Havre and Plymouth, or

Plymouth and Bréhat, he dreamed. I can imagine the furious waves of the Blanchard tidal race giving him the notion of paying homage to the Gulf Stream.

And, as is always the case, scientific facts do not hamper the writer's imagination. He mentions them briefly, then escapes to wherever his fancy takes him.

'Ten days went by in this fashion. Not till May first did the *Nautilus* resume its course due north, after first becoming acquainted with the Lucayos, at the entrance to the Bahama Canal. We were now following the current of the greatest river in the sea, a river that has its own banks, its own fish and its own particular temperature. I refer to the Gulf Stream.

It is indeed a river, flowing freely in the middle of the Atlantic, and its waters do not mix with the oceanic waters. It is a salt river, saltier than the sea around it [...]

The true source of the Gulf Stream, identified by Captain Maury, its point of departure, if you like, is located in the Bay of Biscay. That is where its waters, not as yet remarkable for their temperature or color, begin to gather. It moves down to the south, passes alongside equatorial Africa, heats its waves in the rays of the torrid zone, crosses the Atlantic, reaches Cape San-Roque on the Brazilian coast, and divides into two branches, one of which goes to the West Indies Sea to be further saturated with warm molecules.'

Jules Verne's love affair with the Gulf Stream does not end there. We find him again later on, fascinated by the host of shimmering creatures believed to dwell off those Carolina coasts. And later still, we follow the last voyage of Captain Nemo, to the terrifying seas around the Lofoten Islands ...

↬

The river is within us, the sea is all about us.[6]

5

The Pulse of the Earth

Writing in the 1850s, the American naval officer Matthew Fontaine Murray was the first person to show enthusiasm for this ocean current. Normally factual and utterly detached in his expositions, on this subject he suddenly waxes lyrical:

'The motions of the Gulf Stream [...], beating time for the ocean and telling the seasons for the whales, also suggest the idea of a pulse in the sea, which may assist us in explaining some of its phenomena. At one beat there is a rush of warm water from the equator toward the poles, at the next beat a flow from the poles toward the equator. This sort of pulsation is heard also in the howlings of the storm and the whistling of the wind; the needle trembles unceasingly to it, and tells us of magnetic storms of great violence, which at times extend over large portions of the earth's surface; and when we come to consult the records of those exquisitely sensitive anemometers, which the science and ingenuity of the age have placed at the service of philosophers, we find there that the pulse of the atmosphere is never still: in what appears to us the most perfect calm, the recording pens of the automatic machine are moving to the pulses of the air.

[…]

Now the Gulf Stream, with its head in the Straits of Florida, and its tail in the midst of the ocean, is wedge-shaped; its waters cling together, and are pushed to and fro – squeezed, if you please – by a pressure […], now from the right, then from the left, so as to work the whole wedge along between the cold liquid walls which contain it. May not the velocity of this stream, therefore, be in some sort the result of this working and twisting, this peristaltic force in the sea?'[7]

6

In Which the Author Greatly Regrets Never having Known the Pope

Where does the Gulf Stream stop? As soon as it has crossed the "Mid-Atlantic Ridge" (the chain of volcanic mountains that snakes from one pole to the other beneath the ocean), the current divides and loses its name.

The upper branch, the "North Atlantic Drift," continues on its eastward route and pauses to say hello to Ireland and Scotland before reaching the northern end of Norway.

The lower branches deviate south to join the cold Canary Islands Current. The trade winds are waiting for them at the appointed place. A wind on the quarter, and the waters set off again, westward, to the Caribbean arc and the Gulf of Mexico.

But where, then, does the Gulf Stream begin? Where does it end?

As well ask a circle to name its point of departure and its destination.

༶

If you want to know more about the loop, so my professors at the University of Brest (Ocean Physics Laboratory: Alain Colin de Verdière, Nathalie Daniault ...) had advised me, immerse yourself in the writings of the *Pope*. And when you've done that, go and consult his son.

I considered my Breton friends quite learned enough for me; no need to look elsewhere. Especially because, very close by, near the harbor bottleneck, there existed one of Europe's major oceanographic centers, the French research institute for exploiting the resources of the sea, called from its French initials Ifremer. Its president Jean-François Minster had written a bible related to my subject, *La Machine océan*. It was at Ifremer that Herlé Mercier agreed to give me physics lessons suited to my level (which is to say basic). A little further south the laboratory for studies in space geophysics and oceanography (acronym Legos) brought together the very sharpest minds in the field. And more or less everywhere in France (Paris, Gif-sur-Yvette, Orsay, Grenoble, Roscoff, Vandoeuvre-lès-Nancy, Villefranche-sur-Mer, Sète, Toulon, Aix-en-Provence, Montpellier ...) researchers of world repute made daily additions to our knowledge of the sea. What need had I to cross the Atlantic? Was our own country, France, not underestimating herself once again?

But Alain and Nathalie kept insisting ("The pope taught us all we know," "The pope's son has splendidly developed what his father bequeathed him. And, besides, for someone like you who loves a good story, this man is a real spellbinder ... "); and so I made the acquaintance (via his books) of the pope.

⤻

When the word went out that I intended to pay

my respects to the pope, alias Henry Stommel (27 September 1920 to 17 January 1992), memories, pieces of information, and suggestions came pouring in: "I only met him that one time; he had a really infectious laugh;" "Be sure to mention that he adored his wife, Chickie (Elizabeth); when he wasn't away on one of his ocean trips, he would have lunch with her every day, on the stroke of noon;" "He could paint better than anyone;" "He always went around in worn-out jackets;" "Everybody called him Hank;" "When a question was on his mind, he stopped sleeping and was liable to call you at any hour of the night;" "He never managed to get his doctorate: he founded the association of *non-professional oceanographers* and was its president;" "He was possessed by curiosity, he would go from office to office, asking at each door: 'What's new and interesting today?'" "He studied at Yale for six months to go into the ministry;" "He hated the director of Woods Hole, where he worked, so much that he went off to teach at Harvard. And came back the day after the other fellow left;" etc., etc.

Little by little, a portrait of the pope emerged.

Someone rather like the head of a family, warm-hearted and free-spirited, the incarnation of a bygone era when oceanography could still be practised by "amateurs." Evidently a much-loved man, admired on all sides.

⌒

Stommel was not yet thirty years old. He did not hold any prestigious degree. His work on tides, or on heat exchanges in the atmosphere, had so far stirred no interest. Suddenly, a thunderclap. An article of his was published. Though but a few pages in length, it would lay the foundations for modern dynamic oceanography. Why are currents more powerful on the western slopes of ocean basins? And why does their strength increase with the degree of latitude?

The answer was simple: the influence of Earth's rotation, Coriolis's force.

A few diagrams, a few equations. His colleagues stood slapping their foreheads: why didn't we think of it sooner?

A pope had been born.

No one would ever contest his right to that title. For, as year followed year, Stommel produced new ideas one after another. General explanations, such as the one for chasm circulation: the ocean is more than just a surface. Or more particular explorations: of the circumpolar Antarctic current, for instance, or of some specific spot in the Mediterranean. Land-based studies alternated with ocean journeys. There were some articles that fitted on a single page: "An oceano-graphical curiosity: the perpetual salt fountain." But he also wrote a general survey, *the* general survey on the Gulf Stream.[8]

By way of a break from his scientific labors, the pope would dream up new research tools, notably a kind of unmanned submarine. Such craft, referred to as *gliders*, were built ten years later and they perform invaluable services.

And whenever the sea struck him as rather empty, the pope would invent islands.[9]

7

In Which the Author Journeys to Meet the Pope's Son

There was once, on the coast of North America, a place blessed by the gods: it had inlets, forest, beaches, a profusion of seafood, innumerable fish, and a relatively mild climate, even if ice did occasionally trap boats left at anchor.

Woods Hole: the hole in the woods.

Yielding to its charms, in 1667 the British colonists "bought" this place blessed by the gods from the native Indians.

For the space of two-and-a-half centuries, the new owners would devote themselves to fishing and to the manufacture of tallow candles. There was a brief interval when a processing plant for Chilean guano stank up the atmosphere. It was quickly shut down with the arrival of the first summer people, dazzled by the incomparable, ever-changing beauty of the place. Yachting became popular. Regattas were held. All honor to the winners of these competitions: Captain Harry Pettican, Captain Albert C Swain, Captain Sam Cahoon! Yellowed, spotted photos show them, in blazers and caps, at the helm of *Medora*, *Constance* or *Zaïda*, sloops measuring over fifteen meters. But,within a stone's throw of the library, the Small Boat Museum reminds the visitor that Woods Hole has always been friendly to lighter craft as well, for example the two masterpieces *Rudder* (1897) and *Mucilage* (1903). They illustrate perfectly the sort of toys grown-ups can have.

⌒

Whether at work or at play, Woods Hole has always lived exclusively by and for the sea. Indeed, the name of its main street conveys precisely that information: Water Street, the street leading to the water. And to drive the point home to any visitor who may still not have got the message, it turns out that Water Street is a bridge. On the hour and the half-hour (in summer) or on request (in the off season), the pavement suddenly rises up heavenward to let a small boat go through.

A person interested in the sea and who has come to this spot by chance finds it impossible to leave: nowhere are the waters clearer or as rich.

As far back as 1871, the U.S. government set up its Bureau of Fisheries at Woods Hole. Soon afterward, a marine biology laboratory opened there. (To date, more than fifty Nobel Prize winners have worked at this lab.) In 1930, the Rockefeller Foundation created the Woods Hole Oceanographic Institution (WHOI), which was to become one of the most productive and famous research centers in the world for that field of science. The geologists arrived, soon followed by the teachers: learning about the sea was a national undertaking. The Sea Education Assocation applied itself to the task. The little Indian village turned summer resort was now transformed into a scientific community.

A community disturbed for two months every year by hordes of tourists. For this is the place – alas for Woods Hole! – from which the ferries leave for Martha's Vineyard, that is, for celebrity island. So there is a perfunctory nod and a bow, in passing or perhaps so the kiddies won't be bored, to the sharks, rays, tortoises and other residents of the fine Aquarium at number one Albatross Street. But I can plainly see that people are looking at their watches, with their minds on creatures of a different sort. Once I'm on Martha's island, they're thinking, will I be lucky enough to catch a glimpse of Bill Clinton, Steven Spielberg or Spike Lee?

⌒

Woods Hole.

A hole in the woods.

Quissett campus is a collection of clearings. In the middle of each, stands a brick building. I finally located the one called Clark. The son of the pope is to be found there, on the ground floor, to the left, in room 213, a small office. Needless to say he would protest, guffaw, or even utter thunderous recriminations if he knew the nickname I was giving him. The man, all smiles, now offering me his hand to shake, welcome to the United States, is tall, slender, a youngish athletic sexagenarian, complete with peaked cap, Bermuda shorts and thongs. Hardly the appearance of a pontiff. And yet, by general consent, Phil Richardson is the closest personal friend of the current I am interested in. Having passionately watched it over a period of thirty years, having tracked it along all its courses using every possible device, notably countless drifting buoys, he knows the real facts about this so-called "river."

Let us begin at the beginning.

"Was oceanography, in your case, a calling?"

"No! But I didn't want to be sent to Vietnam."

He went on to explain that he was a construction engineer with no special inclination for marine exploration. But in 1964, rather than go off to war, he joined the crew of a ship assigned to coastal surveying. All day long, he drew maps. A tedious job that left him with the desire to know more. Once back on land, he picked up his studies, doing a Ph.D. at the University of Rhode Island. Then came his arrival at Woods Hole, to begin the long, direct encounter with currents.

Uncertain, he looked at me. It's all very well for this white-haired Frenchman to have presented himself as a novelist; he surely didn't come all this way to hear me talk about my young days.

"Excuse me, but ... What can I do for you?"

"First of all, I would like to know this: where *exactly* does the Gulf Stream start?"

I realized I had put a bit too much emphasis on the adverb *exactly*. In the two years that I had been working on the Gulf Stream, it seemed to me that the current was eluding my grasp more all the time. I felt I was being hoodwinked, deliberately shunted from one track to another. A hundred times, I had heard the totally frustrating sentence: "It's not that simple." It seemed to me that I had the *right* to know for certain. Since I was now face to face with the son of the pope, I was finally about to receive a clear answer. Not just clear, but unalterable.

To be completely frank and take my foolishness as far as it would go, I dreamed of having the pope's son let me in on *the* secret, some location in the Gulf of Mexico that was the precise source of the Gulf Stream, expressed in latitude and longitude, degrees, minutes, and seconds.

The pope's son smiled at me.

"As I see it, the Gulf Stream starts in the Straits of Florida, between the Keys and Cuba. It ends south of the Grand Banks of Newfoundland, just before the Mid-Atlantic Ridge."

I became impatient.

"What about before? What about after?"

"Those are other currents. Of course, you can put a tag saying Gulf Stream on every current in the North Atlantic, but all you'll get out of that is confusion."

I do not recall the rest of the conversation. The expert among experts had not given me the insight I deserved. There was nothing left for me to do but make my escape, with the greatest possible show of courtesy. That is to say, I asked the pope's son for another appointment, to allow myself time for reflection. Would he happen to have some offprints of his articles, to help me palliate my ignorance?

There followed, in my motel (Heritage House, 212 Main Street, Hyannis[10]), forty-eight hours of total immersion. Three times a day, when hunger gained the upper hand, I would surface just long enough to find my way to the dining-room where human whales, men and women, were doing their best to put the finishing touches on their obesity by plundering a buffet that was kept restocked at all hours. One and all, they were exemplars of a void never filled, images of hopelessness.

～

There are few sights more moving than a display of intelligence. I remember my philosophy professors, especially Raymond Aron. I remember that solitary little man, all by himself on the rostrum of the main lecture theater in the Sorbonne, alone against 2,000 students. It was the year after the events of 1968, and people who preferred Tocqueville to Marx and Max Weber to Marcuse were not exactly popular. I remember his blue eyes and that oh so gentle yet implacable voice. The voice, taking its time, was refuting point by point the latest book by Aron's former classmate at the École Normale Supérieure, Jean-Paul Sartre. Soon the solitary little man and his blue eyes vanished. All that remained was a human mind, and it was as though I could see its fragile, superlative mechanisms at work.

I am a map-lover, and now I had thirty years of a cartographer's work around me, scattered all over my bedroom. Plus, by way of a tidbit, the article telling how in 1978 this same Phil Richardson had discovered, among the treasures of the Bibliothèque Nationale, the French national library, nothing less than the first map of the Gulf Stream, the very one drawn by Benjamin Franklin and his cousin Timothy Folger, the Nantucket sea captain. Everyone had been hunting for it unsuccessfully in England and the United States for 200 years, when all the time there was one in Paris. It was a 1786 version, edited during Franklin's long sojourn in France, a country known to have held the American scientist in high esteem, greeting each of his published studies with great enthusiasm.

The discovery of this discovery could not but illumine that Hyannis motel room.

⌇

My subsequent reading would strengthen this sense of wonderment.

A cartographer is a humble person, one that puts all his or her knowledge at the service of a task: describing the world. This is a difficult enough branch of knowledge when one is dealing with *terra firma*, so diverse and unpredictable is the real world. By the time the mapmaker takes on the challenge of portraying the sea, the sea that is the essence of changing, shifting motion, the task becomes ...

An ocean cartographer is a person who casts out buoys, innumerable buoys, some intended to remain on the surface, others meant to reach selected depths. These buoys emit signals that are picked up by satellites. In children's magazines, you often find a game that says: connect up the numbers with lines. You draw a line from the 1 to the 2, from the 2 to the three, and so on. As you do this, a story-book character gradually emerges from what looked like a jumble of numbers. No one played this game more than Phil Richardson. By following the tracks of his buoys, he brought the Gulf Stream to life. A very different Gulf Stream from the one that Franklin and Folger had described. A powerful river, certainly, but unstable, as though tormented by ceaseless regrets or second thoughts. These "regrets," places where the current changes its mind and turns back, are immense, long-lived whirlpools, circles in the water, twenty, thirty, forty kilometers across and, once set in motion, sustained for months in the same circular movement, sometimes clockwise, sometimes anti-clockwise. To the largest ones Phil has given names. Thus, for instance, it is possible to track the birth of Bob, on 9 March 1977, and its westward movement right up to its tragic death. On 1 September, opposite Cape Hatteras, it came dangerously close to the main stream of the current, at about 73°W, 35°N; on the 10th, it was caught in the stream's clutches; ten days later it had disappeared without a trace.

People who have a taste for nautical life stories can also follow the adventurous careers of Dave, Charlie, Arthur, Valentine, and more.

These giant whirlpools are autonomous worlds, each endowed with its own personality. Some are composed of warm water and others of cold; there are those whose waters are salty, and those whose waters are quite fresh. The result is that fish do not find an equal abundance of food in all the whirlpools; they desert the poorer ones to congregate in the vortexes that have more to offer.

꒦

First lesson to be learned from the maps: a portrait of the Gulf Stream is not so much the image of a single hero, the famed broad, majestic river, as it is the picture of a family. The family consists of short-lived individuals: the whirlpools generated by the water's ceaseless movements. Highly diverse currents of energy run through the family. Daily, divisions occur in the family, and daily its members are reunited. The family does not live exclusively on the surface but at every floor of the multi-storied ocean. And every floor has its paths of movement that are often in opposition to those of the other floors. And each of the structure's many stories has its distinct "atmosphere": a certain salinity, a particular pressure, a special temperature. Sometimes floors and ceilings disappear, and the stories mingle.

Land maps, geological maps, go down into the depths, too. But the impression one gets is that they are defining fixed bodies of matter from which the element of time has withdrawn. An ocean map, on the other hand, one that goes down to the abyssal zones, plunges into the living heart of time, of every possible time. It's as though such a map encountered scores of water clocks, a countless horde of as yet invisible time-pieces. Researchers have to construct the faces for these clocks before they can attach the appropriate clock-hands.

⌒

Second lesson emerging from the maps drawn up by Richardson and his colleagues: the birth of the Gulf Stream is not a simple story and, against all expectation, Latin America, too, plays a key role in that birth.

What happens to the fresh, muddy waters of the Amazon once they have reached the sea (16 per cent of all the river water received by the world's oceans)? They are diluted into the south equatorial current, which, coming from Africa, flows back up toward the north-west along the coasts of Guyana and Venezuela to enter the Caribbean Sea.

The sea has a way of making enormous digressions and one of these sent me back to my naïve question about the "source" of the Gulf Stream.

Once again, the explorer of currents had to turn himself into a cartographer. He dropped anchor among the magic islands: Grenada, Saint Vincent, Saint Lucia, Dominica, all those southern gateways through which the great waves rolling in from the open sea sweep into the Gulf of Mexico. For years, on one expedition after another, at the cost of endless dull soundings carried out with stubborn tenacity, Richardson measured the temperature and salinity of the waters. What he found was that more than half of the Gulf Stream's surface waters (from the surface itself to a depth of 100 meters) originate, surprisingly, in the South Atlantic. And, via the Amazon, in a small portion of the Andean snow melt.

No discovery could have moved me more deeply. The walls of my room in that appalling Hyannis motel had disappeared. I was adrift, borne along by this quite recent scientific knowledge and the fierce persistence of memory. It was on the island of Bréhat, where my family had always summered, that I first learned of the Gulf Stream's existence and its (supposed) influence on our near-tropical climate. And it was to Brazil, one of the places where these mild climes originated, that a part of the family had chosen to emigrate following the Second World War.

~

"Go see our harbour," Phil had advised me.

Oceanography may require computers and satellites, but first and foremost it involves boats.

The man in charge of operations greeted me with a long face.

"You're in luck; they're all here, I'm sorry to say."

"Why you're sorry to say?"

"A docked boat isn't being of use to anyone."

The *Atlantis* (85 meters long, crew of thirty-five, and twenty-four scientists) looks like a trawler with the gantry that juts out over its stern. From this hangs a very deep-diving midget submarine, the *Alvin*. The *Oceanus* (54 meters, twelve crew members, for nine researchers on board). The *Knorr* (85 meters, twenty-four sailors, thirty-four scientists). And, still shiny and new, the little newcomer (18 meters), a vessel that was to be used for coastal studies. An impressive fleet.

Any walk along the Institute dock is fraught with peril. Firstly because the dock is encumbered with machines, great big toys such as we have been shown at work on the Moon: robots, mini-platforms, strange antennae-covered spiders poised on long metallic legs.

Dozens of yellow tubes that look like torpedoes add a military note to this unlikely jumble. Take care! The concrete walkway has holes pierced in it, like hatches opening down into the sea. Over each hole sits a crane with a rope dangling down through the opening. It reminds one of those circular holes cut through the ice by Eskimo fishermen. Fish are not the object of this search, but rather fresh proofs of the sea's aggressiveness. From the cranes are suspended guinea-pigs in the form of thermometers, manometers and captors, various movie cameras, tape recorders, every possible device for measuring, each of them protected, encased in armour. Before they are thrown into the ocean, it is important to test their resistance. I wish you could be there when one of these unfortunate machines is hoisted back up out of its forced dip in the sea. Your heart bleeds at the sight of what it and the others have endured. The salt has eaten away at them, rust has devoured them, they have been sucked at by seaweed, colonized by every sort of shell-bearing creature: mussels, barnacles and miniature limpets. And *their* torment had not lasted long, barely a few months.

They had not had to bear the violence of the currents or the pressure of the depths …

Very young people – research workers, graduate students, I was told – did what they could for these survivors: they scraped, patched, repainted, replaced. They were going back and forth between the dock and an immense hangar that looked not so much like a laboratory as it did a giant ship chandlery. There were tongs, shackles, nuts, swivel-hooks; there was copper, steel, stainless steel. Buoys, chains, riggings, the lot.

Here, oceanography showed its true face, a face I had already met in Brest when I visited Ifremer. It is science, no doubt about that. But it is also tinkering and finding expedients. Every institute has its genius at improvisation, its MacGyver, you remember, that TV series hero who always got out of the worst situations by building a helicopter quick as a wink, or a drill that could go through a steel wall, or a telescope for seeing at night. In Brest, the name of the genius who can do these things is Serge Pennec. If he invites you into his house, you'll see what inventiveness really means.

Oceanography is conquest, something not unrelated to war. When certain boats set out on their voyages, are these not referred to as expeditions?

For the sea is jealous of its secrets, revealing them only one at a time, and always grudgingly, always under duress, only when forced to do so by those explorers whose vulnerability in storms is matched by stubbornness in their quest for knowledge: sailors.

⤶

Buoys exist that no one has launched: these are wrecked ships, abandoned vessels that continue to drift, sometimes on the ocean surface, sometimes between two layers of water, and sometimes for years.

In December 1883, the hydrographic service of the U.S. Navy decided to collect systematically the observations of navigators in the North Atlantic. Sailors participated eagerly in this great scientific inquiry. They deposited copies of their log-books in every port: 3,601 reports for the single year 1886 in the port of

New York alone. Washington was the place where all the data received was collated: facts about winds, currents, condition of the sea, obstacles encountered. There, too, monthly maps were drawn up, the famous Pilot Charts (both ways of understanding this name are appropriate: maps drawn by ship's pilots and maps for the use of ship's pilots). On these documents were inscribed the locations of all the wrecks encountered at sea, numbering several hundreds.

It should be understood that at the time, a host of phantom ships littered the Atlantic. In those days, ships were made of wood and remained afloat long after they were wrecked. For many weeks, these hulks drifted, most often standing on end in the water with their stern pointing up at the sky. It need hardly be said that the sight of them struck fear into the hearts of crew members, or that when visibility was poor they represented a serious danger to other ship. More than 400 of these phantoms were identified. Using the mariners' log-books, it was possible to follow their sad, drifting courses month by month, and these courses became so many precious pieces of evidence for those with an abiding interest in currents. Thus it was thanks to floating wrecks that by the end of the 19th century there prevailed a better understanding of the Gulf Stream, of how its path divides as soon as the Stream has passed the Grand Banks of Newfoundland, and how, aside from that, its course describes a vast circle ceaselessly broken by irregularities.

"Look at this."

Side by side, the pope's son and I followed the voyage of the schooner *Twenty-One Friends*, wrecked off Cape Hatteras on 24 March 1885, spotted on 8 August, at 30°W and 55°N, drifting toward Ireland, finally to be swallowed up on 2 December of that year, off Spanish Galicia.

As for the schooner *Fannie E. Welston*, she did not complete the crossing. Abandoned by her crew on 15 October 1891, again in those fearsome approaches to North Carolina, it zigzagged throughout the year 1892 in the south-east Canary Islands before coming back toward the Bermuda Islands, where it saw in the New Year of 1894. The end came ten months later, in the great southern reaches of Nova Scotia.

"And now, what would you say to a little ocean trip?"

⌒

The sloop belonging to the pope's son was anchored in a little harbour at the foot of a sumptuous property bequeathed to the Institute by a billionaire. Billionaires love to bequeath their sumptuous properties to the Institute, as though taking part in exploring the sea made more bearable the prospect of leaving the earth. But this particular billionaire added an awkward condition: he forbade selling the boat; if this condition were breached, the money would go to the local hospital.

Until such time as the Institute figured out what to do with the sumptuous property, my new friend had the use of its landing stage.

And off we went.

On the opposite bank two big sailing ships, the coast-guard training vessels, were being rigged out.

These first post-winter visits aboard are occasions

for the dismayed owner to take stock of all the things that are going to have to be changed or repaired on his or her boat: two starboard turnbuckles, a windlass that has given up the ghost, the boom gooseneck which has somehow managed to get twisted ... More worrisome, there's a bit of play in the tiller.

At times like these, with tension running high, the most obtuse passenger knows he had better keep quiet. Not just refrain from talking but huddle in silence more silent than silence itself. The least sound, a simple reminder of your mere presence, may inspire subdued anger, the kind that results in your never being invited back ...

But it takes more than two or three spots of rust to dishearten a specialist in currents for any length of time. And the north coast of Martha's Vineyard, with its beaches, woods, here and there a few gray houses, was so tranquil that no bad mood could persist.

"Tell me what's happening in Brest."

Evidently "my" Bretons were held in high esteem by this American.

This was the time for me to offer my apologies.

"'Where, I mean really where, does the Gulf Stream begin?' I asked you that on the first day, and I realize now that my question was pretty meaningless."

Without looking at me (his attention was absorbed by another more vital task: he had to guess whether the advancing cloud front was going to force us to take in a reef), Phil Richardson smiled. It was the same smile that I had seen on the face of a lady named Catherine Despeux, one of our most highly regarded Sinologists. To her also I had put a stupid question: what place does the concept of *beginning* have in oriental philosophy? I carried away with me from Woods Hole (the hole in the woods) the following conclusion: when an idiot starts to question them about how or where things *begin*, popes of ocean currents and specialists in Chinese thought have the same way of crinkling their eyes and smiling broadly.

8

Captain Nemo's Grave

Message received and understood: The lesson is clear: the current commonly called the Gulf Stream is merely a segment of a circle. It starts in the Gulf of Mexico and comes to an end shortly after the Grand Banks of Newfoundland.

As they cross the Mid-Atlantic Ridge, that sunken chain of mountains right down the middle of the Atlantic Ocean, the warm waters separate into numerous branches, most of them tending to the south.

But one of the branches stubbornly continues to flow up toward the north-east: this is the North Atlantic Drift.

〜

The tragic ending of *Twenty Thousand Leagues Under the Sea* is well known. With his grand ambition in ruins, sickened once and for all by this world, Captain Nemo chooses a suicide worthy of his immoderate personality. He decides to let his *Nautilus* be swallowed up in the raging waters of the Maelström.

'A single word, twenty times repeated, a terrible word, informed me as to the cause of the agitation that was spreading aboard the *Nautilus*. The wrath of its crew was not directed at *us*!

"Maelström! Maelström!" they were crying. The maelström! Could any name more frightening, in any situation more frightening, smite our ears? Did it mean we were in that dangerous vicinity of the Norwegian coast? Was the *Nautilus* being carried down into the abyss, just when our lifeboat was on the point of tearing loose from her side?

Mariners know that at floodtide,

the waters hemmed in by the Faroe
and Loffode Islands are hurtled forth
with irresistible violence. They form a
whirlpool from which no ship has ever
been able to escape. From every direction
monstrous waves come rushing in. They
form the yawning gulf that is rightly
called the "Belly button of the Ocean,"
and whose power of attraction extends for
a distance of fifteen kilometers. Into it
are sucked not only ships but whales as
well and also the white bears of the Boreal
regions.

To this vortex had the *Nautilus* –
unintentionally or perhaps deliberately
– been committed by her captain. She
was moving in a spiral whose radius was
diminishing further and further. Like her,
the lifeboat still clinging to her side was
being carried along at dizzying speed.
I could sense it. I was experiencing the
secondary whirling sensation that one feels

after a spinning movement that has gone
on too long. We were in a state of terror,
of horror carried to its ultimate degree,
with our blood circulation suspended, the
influence of our nerve system obliterated,
and drenched with bursts of cold sweat
such as accompany the throes of death!
And oh, the noise around our frail lifeboat!
Oh, the roars that echoed for several miles
round about! Oh, the din from those waters
smashing on the pointed rocks of the
ocean floor, where the hardest bodies are
smashed, where tree trunks are worn down
and grow "a hairy coat of fur," to use the
Norwegian expression!

What a desperate plight! We were
thrown around mercilessly. The *Nautilus*
was resisting like a human being. Her
muscles of steel were cracking. From time
to time she would stand straight up and so
would we!

"We must not give up," said Ned, "and

we must tighten the nuts! If we stay with the *Nautilus* we may yet be saved ... !"

He had not finished speaking when there was a loud crack. The nuts were gone, and the lifeboat, torn from its recess, was shot like a stone from a slingshot into the midst of the whirlpool.

I hit my head on an iron rib and the violence of the blow was such that I lost consciousness.'

On his three boats, all named *Saint-Michel*, Jules Verne did a great deal of sailing. But he never personally explored those danger spots in the waters of Norway.

Hence it was in books that he found the information he needed. In books, and certainly in a short story by American writer Edgar Allan Poe: "A Descent into the Maelstrom." It is part of the collection *Tales of the Grotesque and Arabesque*, translated into French by none other than poet Charles Baudelaire, under the title *Histoires extraordinaires*. The French edition dates from 1856, nine years before Jules Verne began work on his *Twenty Thousand Leagues*. An "old man," so runs Poe's narrative, leads some travellers to the mountain top overhanging the current. He tells them how his boat was caught down below in a giant whirlpool. Only by a miracle had he pulled himself free. As a result of his terrifying experience, his hair had turned white. And his beloved brother had disappeared, swallowed up by the monster. The points of resemblance between the two texts are striking, the only difference being that Poe's description, as rendered by Baudelaire, is even more frightening.

Clearly, a visit was called for, as much to honor the memory of Nemo, that misanthropic genius, as to wish the benevolent Gulf Stream a very good day. Its advent saves Norway from the great cold spells that a country at so high a latitude (more than 65°) should by rights be condemned to endure. At the same latitude, Canada is in the grip of ice all year round.

◠

There is a prerequisite to a voyage of that kind: you must choose a boat sturdy enough to brave the elements, when the elements promise to be unbridled. Life's wondrous strokes of fortune (I refer to friendship) offered me a chance to sail on *Vagabond*. I lost no time in heaving my travel bag aboard. They gave me a cabin astern, port side, just under the windpump, whose hum, now languid, now furious, kept me up to date on the force of the wind from start to journey's end.

Vagabond, though young (a scant twenty-six years) and rather short (forty-seven feet), was already a legend. Piloted by France Pinczon du Sel – she is an artist, as well as a former crew member of *Pen Duick III* – and by Éric Brossier, geophysicist and mountain climber, the vessel had, in a period of two years, been around the North Pole, sailing the two mythic "passages" in turn. First they steered their way up along Scandinavia, then made a right turn. Next came 4,000 kilometers of Siberian coast. They wintered in Petropavlovsk, a Kamchatka country spot that deserves to be better known. With the first return of spring they were off again for the Bering Strait. Once again, helm to starboard, and they threaded their way between the ice pack and Alaska, then between the ice and Canada.

Psychiatrically speaking, anyone who has no faith in *Vagabond* would be wiser to stay on land.

There remained the choice of destination, one they could agree on. Jules Verne speaks of "waters hemmed in" by the Faroes and Lofotens. A casual glance at the map will confirm you in the belief that novelists are not to be trusted. Not that they tell outright lies, but they "exaggerate:" the two archipelagos are fully – can you guess? – 600 miles apart.

As the Maelström is a Norwegian *appellation contrôlée*, we headed north-west.

Along the way, there under my windpump (grumbling louder and louder as the days passed), I sought to become better informed.

Looking into dictionaries did not exactly bring me peace of mind. Maelström apparently comes from the old Norwegian word *male*, which means "to churn," to change milk into butter by dint of shaking it.

The stage was set. We could no longer claim not to know the kind of waters we were about to encounter.

~

When Europe and America separated, the future Norway died a thousand deaths. Mountain peaks suddenly surged up, while in other places great chunks of coastline sank out of sight. These upheavals produced the group of Lofoten Islands, some large, others smaller, but all of them mountainous. A green and gray wall in the sea. Near its southern end, this barrier wall developed breaches. That, apparently, was where our maelström had its lair, in those openings, between islets of Røst, Værøy, Mosken and Point Helle, the tip of the larger island called Moskenes.

Impatient to be actually "in the zone," I went endlessly back and forth from reading maps to reading legends, not knowing which would leave me better informed.

'At one time there was the man Værøy

and the woman Mosken. They shared
a cauldron set between their feet. And
night and day, he with a staff, she with a
ladle, they stirred. Not wildly, but never
stopping. Such is the law of cookery. The
best of understanding prevailed between
the man and the woman.

Now, what should they see one night
by the light of the full moon but seven
brightly shining figures walking upon the
sea.

"You should go and look," said the
woman. (For all eternity she would regret
making her suggestion.) "Perhaps someone
is trying to steal our fish."

Mumbling and grumbling, the man
left his seat. The next moment he was filled
with wonder. The seven figures were seven
young women, much younger than Mosken
and stunningly beautiful. And to crown
their allure, they were almost weeping,
they were imploring.

"Oh dear, oh dear, oh dear! We have lost our crowns of moonlight! Who will help us find them?"

What would you have done in the man Værøy's place?

He returned extremely late, to find the woman Mosken beside herself.

"A fine hour you've chosen to be coming back!"

To vent her rage, she was moving her ladle around very hard in the cauldron.

The man Værøy replied that he had nothing, absolutely nothing to be sorry for. He, too, was gripped by anger. He plunged his staff into the cauldron. Soon the cauldron became a very hell: huge waves, deep whirlpools, sprays of foam.

The maelström had been born.

Naturally, the man Værøy and the woman Mosken were finally reconciled. Their movements became gentler and so the turmoil in the cauldron subsided.

But with every full moon, jealousy
returns to torture the woman Mosken when
she remembers the seven beautiful women.
Her ladle begins once again to beat the
ocean. The man Værøy answers back.
And there is hell once more.'

The first texts mentioning the Maelström go back
to the 16th century.

In a kind of geographic diary that he called
My Gothic Charter, Swedish bishop Olaus Magnus
writes:

'Between Røst and Lofot is an abyss so
deep that it can suddenly swallow up the
traveller. Captains who sail there lose all
control of their ships. [...] The forces of
nature at work in that vicinity surpass,
beyond all possible dispute, the elemental
violence to be met in Sicily's Charybdis or
at all the other known places in the world
[...]. Many men of learning have striven

in vain to find the explanation for these phenomena. They have concluded that some sort of divine power must be present there.'

Erik Hansen Schonnebøl, bailiff of the Lofotens, hence someone who knew the area well, agrees:

'When a contrary wind rises, the maelström becomes so turbulent and makes so much noise that the land and walls of Helle farm shake [...]. The very whales are swept into the vortex. Numerous are the bodies of dead whales discovered along our shores [...].'

This infernal phenomenon gave rise to a whole body of literature, including a poem by Peter Dass, a pastor and traveller in those parts toward the end of the 17th century.

'When the moon is full or the sky is hidden

*A roaring is heard that fills you with fear and
     distress
Shivers of fear begin to run up your back*

*And whosoever then puts out to sea
Will soon behold nothing more nor fear a living
     soul
For his only grave will be a hole in the water.'*

The bad repute of this spot had quickly spread
throughout the Atlantic world. American writer Poe
had no lack of violent currents close to home, and his
short life (1809–49) did not permit of his travelling
to Norway, yet it was the Maelström that he chose to
describe.

Thus it was with a certain degree of apprehen-
sion that *Vagabond* drew close to the southernmost
point of the Lofoten Islands. As expected, the weather
was beginning to deteriorate. Slowly but surely, the
barometer was falling; 1.012 hectopascals; 1.010;
1.007. We could take it as a sign that the anticyclone,
which had accompanied us thus far, was now leaving

us, to go and protect other ships less presumptuous than ours. As though it had been waiting a long time for someone to open the door, the wind had begun to blow, freshening and bent on revenge. The sky was not falling on our heads, not yet, but our crow's-nest, installed level with the crosstrees of the topmast and very useful for spotting growlers, would soon disappear from sight into the clouds. For the time being, the clouds were content merely to swallow up the tops of any islets we encountered.

At the beginning of August, the Norwegian night is just barely starting its training program for the coming winter. The night is showing its strength but not yet putting that strength to use. It nibbles away at the daylight without much conviction. And then it stops when it comes to the half-light. You can still see. In order for the horizon to disappear, mist or rain has to be involved.

On this false-darkness night, the mist and rain toyed with us, showing us Værøy Island, shortly after that Mosken Island, only to hide both isles from our view a moment later. Their message was easy to understand: Okay, you are indeed in the area of the Maelström. Don't let that fool you into thinking you have any control whatsoever over events.

Most lighthouses in Norway look like toys, cute little white turrets with a red hat on top. This one is called Lofotoden and right after it comes a sheer cliff. In no time at all, our vessel had rolled twice (foresail wrapped around its stay, mainsail hugging the mast), we had taken time to enjoy a favorite sailors' song, announcing a completed stage in the journey – no more jolts and heaves, the longed-for sleep and rest – we had heard the joyful clank of the chain running out fast through the hawsehole, and *Vagabond* was dozing off, a stone's throw away from the monster.

On the other side of a rock was the famous Helle farmhouse, the one whose walls shake when the Maelström is having a fit of rage.

Vagabond has a flat hull, enabling her to pass over ice. This means that with the slightest current of air she slides and travels around her anchor. Like a certain revolving crêpe restaurant built at the top of the water tower in Ploudalmézeau in North Finistère, she's a ship that will bend over backwards (turn in a circle would be more appropriate) to make sure you see the world. By one in the morning, dawn had broken. Through my tiny porthole under the windpump, I could see the white lamp of Lofotoden lighthouse. Then the cliff with its steep face. Then a pebbly little beach down to which ran something resembling a road, a casual affair, consisting of ill-fitting stones, probably used from time immemorial to drag fishermen's boats up the beach to a dry place. Finally, a segment of open sea that seemed to be running streaked with foam: the Maelström ...

And once again, lighthouse, steep cliff ...

Sometimes, *Vagabond* would rotate in the other direction. Current, rock, beach ...

Always the same landmarks, like the numbers on a clock face.

But how is a person supposed to sleep in the middle of a clock that doesn't know which way the time is passing?

⌒

Next day, the sky was grey to westward and blue to the east. The Lofotens were a mountainous wall stopping the clouds.

The sea does not like having appointments made for it. Nothing is more foreign to its nature than to put on a programmed display of terrors for an audience. The sea is not a wild beast in a circus. No one will ever tame the sea. So a Frenchman had come from far away to shudder at the show, had he? Well, the sea had a little trick of its own saved up for him.

And yet we had foreseen every contingency. We knew the exact time of half-tide, the precise moment of the advertized apocalypse. So our hearts were pounding as we weighed anchor and left our haven.

This was right at the foot of the mountain where Edgar Allan Poe had placed his bruised and broken hero.

And then nothing happened.

Blue sky, calm sea.

An Irish hurricane, as the English say. Just a few eddies here or there, soon absorbed by a long, peaceful swell.

Vagabond refused to believe it. *This* was the Maelström?

Vagabond is not a collectivity to be trifled with. *Vagabond* rejected disillusionment. She held out for a long time, ferreting around between the islets of Tjeldholmen, Buholman, Langrumpholmen and others, like a big dog furious at not flushing out any game. But there was nothing there. A peaceful expanse, virtually undisturbed, just a few flecks of foam scattered here and there. Between Béniguet and Bréhat, that dear Kerpont current of my childhood in Brittany had presented me with far choppier seas than this.

I could quite happily have lain at anchor right there in the midst of the so-called deadly perils, waiting for them to show signs of life.

But *Vagabond* had other plans. I could feel her shrugging her shoulders. "Whatever people say, ocean currents are not a very great matter." She set sail to the north, toward Spitzbergen, where she would find ice fields awaiting her, adversaries worthy of her mettle.

As can well be imagined, there was no lack of

derision from the crew. In vain did I show them the marine instructions; I was wasting my time. I was the butt of many a gibe, my tormentors being made more inventive by the evening ration of whisky. As an occupation, hunting sea currents has its highs and lows; this was a low.

Your time will come, reader, never fear. I refused to end the Maelström adventure on that note, on a fiasco. I did return to Norway, and I shall soon be telling you all about the Saltstraumen, a twenty-knot current.

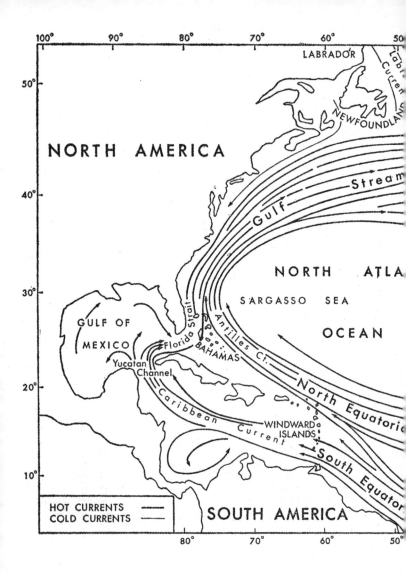

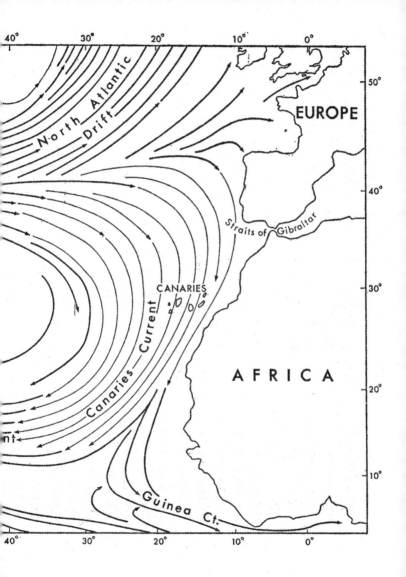

III
Mapping the Sea

"The Bureau of Longitudes is assigned the task of editing *La Connaissance des Temps*, the weather information bulletin, which shall be printed at the expense of the French Republic."

1

Tribute to an Admiral

From time immemorial, sailors have cast bottles into the sea ...

... in an attempt to breach their solitude ...

... and also to map the course of the currents.

Maury describes the ruling passion of a certain Admiral Beechey. In the course of his journeys, he would throw bottles overboard, bottles by the hundred, bottles by the thousand. Then he would wait impatiently for news of them (he had created an unbelievable network of informers, all up and down the Atlantic coast).

One of his bottles, thrown overboard in 1837 at Cape Horn, was found twenty years later in Ireland.

Another, thrown into the open sea off Dakar, was picked up on a beach in Guernsey.

While the course followed by the first of these two bottles caused the admiral great perplexity, the itinerary of the second bottle confirmed him in the belief that the Gulf Stream was a loop.

2

A Tribute to Prince Albert the First of Monaco (1848 – 1922)

In the course of his long life, including a thirty-three year reign, this Prince's interests ranged over:

– photography and the newly emerging art of the cinema (as early as 1896, he bought a motion-picture camera);
– cycling (a regular practitioner of long-distance bicycle trips, he often cycled from Paris to Monaco);
– automobiles (he started the Monte-Carlo Rally in 1911);
– opera and dance (he was a close friend of Diaghilev);
– aviation (his first experience of flight was in Santos Dumont's dirigible; in 1912

he flew over his Principality aboard a
"hydroaeroplane"; he financed Maurice
Léger's helicopter, one of the first aircraft of
that species);
— speedboat racing;
— justice (he allied himself with the pro-
Dreyfus camp very early on);
— marriage (he would have two wives);
— mutual benefit insurance (he chaired its
world congress) and peace (he established an
'international institute' whose aim was to
promote the practice of arbitration).

'One of the most desirable of all
goals pursued by civilization,
namely eliminating brutal rivalries
based on the right of the strongest
and leading to murderous wars,
ruin, and suffering, is perhaps
concealed behind the Mutual
Benefit movement, which,
combined with Arbitration,
could give rise to new modes of

human behavior. Arbitration and
mutuality, we could not offer
a surer guaranty of humanity's
progressive march toward complete
civilization, for when human beings
have formed the habit of mutual
aid, they may well lose that of
mutual destruction.'

But his first passion was the sea.

He learned to sail in the navy, first the French navy,
then the Spanish. From that time forward, he would
never stop exploring the seas, buying or commission-
ing the construction of larger and larger boats: the
Hirondelle (32 meters), the *Princess Alice* (53 meters),
the *Princess Alice II* (73 meters), and the *Hirondelle II*,
his most splendid toy, completely devoted to oceanographic research (82 meters).

Over a period of forty years he would ply the
waters of the Atlantic, sometimes with nets of his
own invention, fishing for new species (including
the *Grimaldichthys profundissimus*, pulled forcibly

from 6,000 meters below the surface), sometimes launching kites to scan the clouds more closely. In his marine activity, he had a predilection for tracking down currents.

Long before him, other people had taken an interest in natural flotsam. Among the first was none other than Columbus, who, in preparation for his famous crossing, collected all the first-hand reports available containing references to pieces of foreign wood, or exotic seeds and nuts picked up on the beaches of Madeira or Portugal. Scotland, the Faroe Islands, Iceland and Norway have long been familiar with these sorts of harvest.

But throwing bottles into the sea for serious scientific purposes had to await the early 19th century before it became a common practice.

⌐

Albert had the resources to launch these bottle campaigns on a scale not previously seen. Inside each floater a message had been enclosed, drafted in seven languages. The French text read: "Dans le but d'étudier les courants …

> ' … In the interests of studying ocean
> currents, this paper has been thrown
> into the sea, on the initiative of Professor
> Pouchet, and with the participation of
> the City Council of Paris, pursuant to
> its resolution of March 16, 1886, during
> the third scientific expedition of the
> Monagascan yacht *Hirondelle* under the
> command of His Highness the Hereditary
> Prince of Monaco. – Any person finding
> this paper is asked to see that it reaches
> the authorities of his or her country to be
> transmitted to the French Government,
> with a description of the circumstances in
> which this paper was found.'
>
> Albert First, King of Monaco
> G. Pouchet, Professor at the Museum of Paris

And the other languages followed:

Нашедшаго сию бумагу лросят
лослатъ таковую Морскому
Веломству своей страны
для передачи Фрамиузскому
Мравитељству.

'Den person, som måtte finde dette papir,
anmodes om at overlevere det til bane
Havde Marine Ministerium for at blive
tilstillet den Franske Regjering'

'Any one finding this paper is requested
to remit it to the Naval Authorities of his
country, in order to be forwarded to the
French Government.'

'Jeder, der dieses Papier findet, wird
erfordert dasselbe an die Seebehörde seines
Landes zu übermachen zur Übertragung an
die französische Regierung.'

'De vinder van dit papier wordt verzocht,

het zoopoedig mogelijk afte geven aan de
Maritime Overheid, onverschillig in welk
land, om bet aan de Fransche Regeering te
doen opzenden.'

'Se ruega á quien encuentre este papel que
lo remita a la Autoridad maritima de su
pais, para que sea tramitido al Gobierno
Frances.'

'Roga se a quem achar este papel, que tenha
a bem remettelo a Auctoridade maritima
da sua nação, para que seja trasmettido ao
Governo Francez.'

And the Prince himself assessed the achievement of
his four campaigns.

'The study of this current [the Gulf Stream]
marked the beginning of my career as an
oceanographer in 1885. At that time I
launched scientifically constructed floaters

numbering in all 1,675, along several lines between Europe and America. Each of these contained a soldered glass tube in which a message had been enclosed, written in several languages and asking that the person into whose hands it might fall arrange for it to be sent to me with information as to the place and date of the finding.

Sixteen per cent of these objects have been returned to me. A great number of them, starting their journey from the vicinity of Newfoundland, were scattered along the coasts of Europe as far as Gibraltar, on the African coast as far as the Canary Islands and the Cape Verde Islands. Others were found later in the West Indies and on the coasts of Central America. Briefly, by comparing the order in which the floaters reached shore and the lengths of time their journeys took, I found it possible to reconstruct on a map the whirlpool formed by this great current,

and even to state approximately the speed
at which it moves along several segments
of its course.'

⌇

Since that time, the bottles have become more
sophisticated. Some of them drift, as before. Others
are anchored at depths of up to 4,000 meters by two
tons of locomotive wheels (the least expensive ballast).
Most are little robots. Some of them are little submarines: they dive, fish deep down, and, on stated days,
come back up to surrender their booty.

Nostalgia is apt to make us feel sorry that the
modern bottles no longer contain artistically penned
love letters, but rather numbers, lists of numbers.
Satellites, as they pass overhead, collect up these
numbers like water utility inspectors who come with
a pencil behind their ear to read the meter.

3

Eyes in the Sky

4 October 1957. The classroom door opens. Our school principal appears, looking like a man who has seen a vision.

"On your feet, gentlemen! This is a historic day. The Russians have just launched a satellite around the Earth. It is called Sputnik. Three cheers for Science! You may be seated."

And with that he is gone.

We look at each other. What's a satellite? We have all just turned ten. In the silence, we hear another door open, the door of the classroom next to ours. "On your feet, gentlemen!"

Obviously another fact we didn't know was that July 1st of this same year marked the beginning of the International Geophysical Year, in other words, that the greatest scientists had held an assembly where they decided to join forces and give new impetus to the exploration of an unknown entity: the Earth. For in truth, knowledge of the Earth had scarcely progressed since ancient times. The most basic information was lacking. Especially lacking was a starting point, an overview.

The launching of Sputnik supplied the answer: from space, man would finally be able to see his planet. This age-old dream was realized a few years later. Thanks to the Apollo astronauts whose mission paved the way for the Moon walk, a globe heaved into view out of the night. It was our globe.

~

5 July 1983. Pasadena, California.

A group of French engineers, feeling intimidated, walk into a place they have heard so much about that it has a mythic aura: the Jet Propulsion Laboratory. This is where the probes for exploring the outer limits of the solar system were designed. So was the

121

first satellite for use in maritime observation, Seasat. The lab embodied excellence in the field of human curiosity.

The French visitors were members of CNES, the Centre national des études spatiales; the Americans belonged to NASA. Government ministers in both countries had requested that they curtail their expenses, which meant ... they had better work together.

They would comply, though reluctantly at first.

The child of their joint endeavors took to the air from Kourou in French Guyana on 10 August 1992. It had a double baptismal name: Topex – that was the American designation, from Ocean Topography Experiment – and Poseidon, from *Plate-forme océa-nographique de surveillance et d'études intégrées de la dynamique de l'océan et de son niveau*, oceanographic platform for surveillance and integrated studies of the ocean and its level; – that was the French choice.

Intended not to take its eyes off the sea for three full years, Topex-Poseidon in fact continued its scrutiny for twelve years, never abating the keenness of its gaze.

The first portraits of our planet as seen looking down from above were photos. Then motion-picture cameras took over. By definition, a working satellite does not come back down to earth. Hence recovering the rolls of film was not the easiest part of the procedure: a variety of techniques would be used, all of them derived from the old-fashioned butterfly net.

As may well be imagined, non-military ocean surveillance did not have a high priority. The Cold War was uppermost in everyone's mind and in everyone's budget. Satellites focused their attention only on non-submerged land masses and on whatever warlike disturbances those land masses might reveal.

In the late 1970s, however, we humans remembered that the sea, too, existed ... and that it governs our lives. We commanded our watchful robots to look at bodies of salt water as well.

The result was stunning: within a few days, more information was collected than had been accumulated by sailors over thousands of years.

It all happened as though, viewed from high up, the sea was suddenly defenseless and had no choice but to reveal a goodly portion of its mysteries, items such as its color, so variable depending on the region and the time of year, its surface temperature, the velocity of the winds blowing across it ... and also the habits of certain animals.

Leatherback turtles, an endangered species, are born in French Guyana, then take to the sea. Whither bound? Little markers were pasted onto their scales. And we now know that they cross the Atlantic, with a predilection for the whirlpools of the Gulf Stream.[11]

❧

But the sea's biggest secret is its *height*. And only a satellite can measure height continuously across all of the oceans. It is no longer a case of 20,000 leagues under the sea, but twenty million leagues above the sea. Once the secondary eddy of the waves has been factored out, the measurements taken by a satellite, with their precision correct to the nearest centimeter, enable scientists to pinpoint zones where water accumulates. In the Gulf of Mexico, the Atlantic is higher than it is elsewhere. And in the Labrador sea, for example, significant low areas have been noted.

And just as we read Braille by running our fingers over reliefs, so these humps and hollows tell us about the tides, currents, and whirlpools. They even enable us to map the ocean floor.

You will understand why the *height* of the sea is considered in oceanography as an *integral magnitude.* Height has the same general capacity for explaining the ocean as pressure has when it comes to talking about the atmosphere.

～

So, for going on thirty years, man has been launching eyes into the sky to have them watch the sea. Will the eyes close? I'm afraid they may. The satellites are getting older. If a decision to replace them is not made soon enough, there will come a time when the watch is interrupted for lack of watchers. Decades of effort will be ruined, at least in part. Curiosity is valuable if it has continuity, and also if it remains permanently unsatisfied: can anyone be content to observe the surface of the sea without seeking obstinately to explore its depths as well?

What makes an eye useful is that the observer, as well as understanding the pieces of information received, can interpret their significance and if need be sound the alarm.

A week after the earthquake in the Indian Ocean, my scientist friends from the Club des Argonautes came round to my house. They set up their projector. On one of my walls there appeared the data supplied by satellites on the morning of 26 December 2004.

What I saw, in place of the photos that normally brighten up that wall, was a film of the tragedy.

4

In Praise of Models

The American scientist Lewis Fry Richardson had a single obsession: he wanted to predict the weather. And it infuriated him not to have available the power of calculation needed to achieve his ambition. So he had dreams. In 1914, he conceived the idea of assembling in a vast hangar 64,000 people, all highly proficient in mathematics. His plan had to be abandoned. But he predicted: "Perhaps one day, in the remote future, we will be able to calculate faster than time is moving … ." Fifty years later, with the advent of the first models, his dream became a reality.

A scale model is a small copy of something, with the proportions kept. Such a model consists of pieces, any one of which can be removed to study the consequences of removing that component. Gibraltar, for instance. If we close the Strait, what changes do we note in the circulation of Atlantic waters? Or, let us assume that the Arctic ice-fields start to melt faster than before. How will the Gulf Stream's rate of flow be affected?

A model is dynamic. It will serve to complete the data – never adequate – supplied by observation. As of 19 December 2004, within the scope of the Argo network, the measurer satellites were receiving information from only 1,544 floaters. Just 1,544 witnesses to report on the never-ending spectacle, across their surfaces and down into their depths, of the five oceans!

Without the satellites, who would gather these data?

But without a model, who would link them up?

The mechanisms of the sea are too complex and the field of observation too hostile and too vast. Unless technologies are compatible and nations are cooperating, no advances can be made. Oceanography – and this is one of its major teachings – compels countries to form alliances, or at least the kinds of alliance stimulated by competition.

American universities at Princeton and Miami, and the Massachusetts Institute of Technology, remain at the forefront in developing numerical models. But France has not been left behind. Anyone who knows at first hand the subdividing and susceptibilities of French government departments can only bow reverently to the ocean. The ocean must have been much loved and its mysteries must have exercised great fascination in order for a group to emerge, a group declared to be of value to the nation, in which the public weather office, the national scientific research center, the naval oceanographic service, the sea research institute, the research and development institute and the space studies center[12] all deign to participate! The results have justified these surrenders of sovereignty a hundred times over. Thanks to the Mercator model, the ocean comes to life before your very eyes. You can see in technicolor the circulation of its waters and the way their temperature, salinity and direction change here and there, day after day ...

The scientific types try in vain to curb your enthusiasm ("Those images aren't real, y'know; they're just simulations.") You feel at once childlike (the wonder of it all) and godlike (you are looking down upon it from a great height).

The work goes on. As images achieve higher definition, phenomena that are increasingly local in scope can be incorporated into the models and their role in the overall world circulation of waters more and more exactly analyzed. And yet, the tumultuous relationship between the sea and the atmosphere has so far revealed only a minuscule part of its secrets. Hence we find meteorologists and oceanographers urging each other to quicken the pace in their respective fields. If this group or that group drags its heels, neither lot will further its knowledge, that is, its ability to predict.

And all the time, as though honoring Lewis Fry Richardson's dream, the power to calculate never ceases to grow. The last time I went for my physics lesson from Herlé Mercier of Ifremer in Brest, the office next to his was empty. His colleague had gone off to Japan:

no other computer in the world could help him solve a particular problem that had to do with a particular condition of certain marine whirlpools.

The Bureau of Longitudes, Arago, and the Argonauts

Addresss? Number 23, Quai de Conti, Paris, on the bank of the Seine, opposite the Louvre Museum.

Yes, it's a palace; it was even built by Le Vau, the architect who designed Versailles.

Pay no attention to the protests of your shyness; walk in.

First courtyard, second courtyard. At the far end of courtyard three is a small building. You have arrived.

The Bureau was created on the seventh of Messidor, year III of the Revolutionary Calendar (25 June 1795). The people's representative, Father Grégoire, addressed the Convention government as follows:

'I stand before you, as spokesman for your Committees of the Navy, Finance, and Public Education, to propose the establishment of a Bureau of Longitudes.

An account of the reasons prompting such a request will show what an indispensably necessary tool this Bureau will be for making our Navy prosper.

Themistocles said "Whoever is master of the sea is master of the land." One of our poets expressed the same idea in his own way: "Neptune's trident is the scepter of the world."'

Article 5 of the text establishing the Bureau provides as follows:

'The Bureau of Longitudes is assigned the task of editing *La Connaissance des Temps,* the weather information bulletin, which shall be printed at the expense of the French Republic. It will improve the

astronomical tables and the methods used
in dealing with longitudes and will concern
itself with the publication of astronomical
and meteorological observations [...]'

This Bureau was the agency that sent François Arago to the Balearic Islands in 1806 to complete the measurement of our meridian. Taking advantage of the Spanish war, which put an end to the project, he sailed the sea, measuring everything that came his way.

The sea would remain his preoccupation. Later (1848), he was even made Minister of the Navy. His concern with matters maritime was always practical. How could progress in optics be used to improve the spotting of reefs? How could better knowledge of winds and currents help prevent (to the extent possible) shipwrecks and reduce sailing times (from fifty days to twenty-nine for the trip from New York to Rio de Janeiro)?

Following sound geodesic principles, he realized that contrary to earlier belief, we cannot explain major currents by the changes in level on the bottom of the sea. With visionary insight, he preferred to look for an explanation by studying disparities of saltiness and temperature from one water zone to the next. And he was already interested in tracing the paths of deep currents ...

Arago was director of the Bureau of Longitudes from 1834 to 1853.[13]

Every Thursday, on my way to the weekly sitting of the Académie française, I would go past that mythic place, that most legendary observatory of our planet and its liquid component. Then a day came when I dared open the door and go up to the second storey.

There were ten learned men around a table, and they were expecting me. They represented all the disciplines concerned with the ocean. They included researchers and engineers; most of them were both. Ten men with a passion, who had decided to go on working in spite of retirement. They were the Club des Argonautes.[14]

They listened as I presented my impudent project: "I love the sea and its currents. But I really know nothing about them. I would like to tell their story."

They didn't sneer or scoff. They nodded their heads. They looked at one another.

Subsequently, under the patronage of Arago, they attempted to instil, into the head of the poor, ignorant novelist, a few basic ideas, starting with this message:

Planet Earth is a spaceship. Human activity can make life on board pure hell. We must learn to fly the ship the best way possible. Let us stop being mere passengers and become *geonauts* instead.

IV
The Great Aquarium

"He was an old man who fished alone in a skiff in the
Gulf Stream."
Ernest Hemingway, *The Old Man and the Sea*

1

The Fertility of Whirlpools

For Jules Verne the Gulf Stream is nothing more or less than an aquarium, the richest one on the planet. Into the aquarium he empties a whole dictionary.

'This current carried along within it a whole world of living creatures. Argonauts, so common in the Mediterranean, travelled with the current in large schools. Of cartilaginous sea-dwellers, the most remarkable were the skate, which, with their very agile tails making up one third of their bodies, presented a vast diamond shape twenty-five feet long; then, small dogfish a meter in length, with big heads,

short, rounded snouts, pointed teeth
arranged in several rows and bodies that
appeared to be covered with scales.

Among the bony fish, I noted some of
the grey wrasse peculiar to these waters,
sea-bream whose irises sparkled like
fire, meter-long sciaena, their wide jaws
bristling with little teeth and uttering
a faint cry, black centronotes of which I
have spoken previously, blue coriphenes
trimmed in gold and silver, parrot-fish,
truly the rainbows of the ocean, that
for color can compete with the most
gorgeous tropical birds, boskian blennies
with triangular heads, bluish rhombs,
completely scaleless, batrachoideans
covered with a transverse yellow band
forming a Greek t, hordes of swarming
little gobies covered with brown spots,
dipterodons with silvery heads and yellow
tails, various representatives of the salmon
family, mugilomores, slender-bodied,

shining with a reddish-brown luster, that
Lacépède dedicated to his amiable life's
companion, and finally the American
knightfish, a handsome creature, decorated
with every noble order and bedecked with
every sort of ribbon, found on the shore of
that great nation where ribbons and noble
orders are held in so little esteem.'

Let us acknowledge the novelist's lively style and
come back to reality, which also has its merits.

To convince us that such is the case, another
digression proves to be necessary, one just long enough
to answer this little question: what is life?

The answer seems simple at first. In order for life
to appear, there have to be water, carbon, nutritive
salts (nitrogen-, phosphorus-, or silicon-based), and
energy (sunlight or hot springs). Is that sufficient?
Would a robot immersed in such an environment
acquire *life*? That is another problem and a huge one.
Let us continue.

In the sea, there is no shortage of water, as La

Palice[15] would have said. Nor of carbon: the sea is saturated with it.

The difficulty arises from the thickness of the ocean. The sun brings light only to the ocean's upper layers. The nutritive salts come from the remains of animals that have died, that is, sunk. So, in the words of the song, the sun has a date to meet someone who isn't there. If the sun's energy does not make contact with the salts that carpet the bottom of the sea, life will not emerge.[16]

At the surface level of the oceans, on the other hand, the presence of chlorophyll, an energy fixative, is a sign that the synthesis is taking place, hence that living matter is being produced.

Satellites have made it possible to draw a map of the world's supply of chlorophyll. And just as on dry land there are deserts and forests, so there are to be found on the surface of the sea zones that are completely sterile and others that are veritable meadows: in these zones grow plants (phytoplankton), that will be greedily devoured by animals (zooplankton), on which fish feed.

Here endeth the digression. The whirlpools, bless them, can now make their entrance.

Theoretically, there is nothing about the Gulf Stream that should make it specially attractive to fish. Since it is a current of warm water, it is relatively poor in food.

One can understand why certain large creatures, marlin and swordfish for instance, would enjoy swimming in these fast-moving waters where they can give full play to their muscles. Lesser species, however, have to think mainly about sustenance.

Its biological resources do not, then, account for the current's role as "bringer of fertility" to the ocean, and we must seek the explanation elsewhere. The Gulf Stream is in the first instance a *force*: eighty-five million cubic meters per second at Cape Hatteras, a torrent anywhere from fifty to a hundred kilometers in width and a thousand meters in depth. The Atlantic is not about to receive such a guest without experiencing a few upheavals.

From the Straits of Florida to Cape Hatteras, the course is fairly regular. It is bounded on the left by the continental shelf: this is the shallows (average depth: 200 meters), an extension of the American coasts. Obviously, power of that magnitude cannot accept constraint without balking. So to show its independence, from time to time the Gulf Stream moves away from the shelf, but comes back before too long. These meanderings have beneficial consequences. The deviations act as a summons: waters will come welling up from the depths, along the slope of the shelf, bringing with them nutritive substances. A food chain is created; local species, the menhaden (a kind of herring) and the impressive bluefish, will find food here in abundance.

After Cape Hatteras things get serious. The Gulf Stream veers to the right, leaves the shelf that it had been using as an embankment, and takes to the open sea. Undersea landscape features will continue to influence its route, notably the line of mountains that, at great depth, link Cape Cod to the Mid-Atlantic Ridge.

The meanderings expand until they form the whirlpools referred to earlier. These whirlpools soon separate from the main stream and will have a crucial influence on the ocean's biology. It was long believed that the Gulf Stream was a virtually impassable barrier between the North and South Atlantic, a belief based on a misunderstanding of the role played by those whirlpools.

The northern edge of the Gulf Stream meets the icy Labrador Current, making the whirlpools into rings of warm water surrounded by cold water. Spinning clockwise, they confine the nutritive substances in the lower depths. The fish are quick to abandon these ungenerous zones.

On the south edge, in contrast, whirlpools form that are colder than the surrounding environment. They are spinning counter-clockwise, which encourages food to rise back toward the surface. That is how the Sargasso Sea becomes "fertilized."

Readers of either sex, who without making long journeys would like confirmation of what I say, have only to stick a teaspoon into a cup of tea. Let them stir with the teaspoon, first one way then the other. They will see how the dregs, the bits of tea-leaf that have escaped the strainer, rise up or go down to the bottom.

2

Journeys and Metamorphoses of the Eel

One of the sixteen species of eel, the European one (*Anguilla anguilla*), is a daughter of the Sargasso Sea. That is where its egg comes into the world, at a depth between 400 and 700 meters, in water whose temperature does not exceed 17° C. When it has grown up, and then been baptized – by the French – with the pretty name *feuille de saule*, willow-leaf (one can also say leptocephaloid), it comes back up to the surface, where it feeds on zooplankton, food which, as we have seen, owes its own existence in part to the cold whirlpools of the great current.

The Gulf Stream will not stop with this initial gift. Sensing that the newly hatched eel needs to travel, the current will lend its might to the creature, carrying the eel along in its flow. The willow-leaf can float, but has not yet learned to swim.

Off the coast of France, its first destination, the eel leaves the kindly current that has transported it thus far, turns aside into the estuaries and mutates into an elver, much prized by the gourmets of that country, who call it a *civelle* or a *pibale*.[17]

If the young eel manages to escape the fishermen's nets, a new existence begins. For some ten years, the creature will live in fresh water. It has now metamorphosed into a long, yellow fish. The eel will benefit from a more settled way of life: it may reach 150 centimeters, for a weight of four kilograms ...

But our eel will hear once more the call of distant journeys. We are now at the end of summer, somewhere in the last days of August or perhaps even into September. Putting all other concerns aside, the creature must head back to the open sea. For it must now breed, and as a place to breed, no river strikes the eel as worthy; only the Sargasso Sea will do.

But the voyage is a long one.

Once again, the Gulf Stream – or at any rate

its southern branches, the Canary Islands Current, followed by the Equatorial Current – offers its services.

In preparation for the special event, the eel has put on a new dress. The fish is now silver, and dives downward to the deepest reaches. Specialists are of the opinion that the pressure encountered at those depths revive the creature's sexuality. Short of trying the method out for oneself, who shall say they are mistaken?

3

The Codfish and the Atmosphere

Of one thing we can be certain: the codfish thrives on conflict. She really feels at the top of her form only at the *fronts*, those choppy zones where the sea comes into collision with the upward motion of waters from the ocean floor (the Grand Banks, Iceland, the Lofotens), where cold water masses meet warm ones.

These disturbances, that send nutritive salts rising back up from the depths to the light of day, are like so many food pantries.

More difficult to explain are the fluctuations in fish population. Why, at certain periods, are cod so rare that there is fear they may become extinct? And why do they suddenly come back in great numbers?

No cod unless there is plankton. And no plankton unless the water is right. But the mother of water is the sky. For its temperature, and for the ordering of its layers, water is dependent on the circulation of the atmosphere ... which in turn is cyclical (a "North-Atlantic oscillation," of which we shall hear more). And yes, the demographic variations of the codfish do correspond to those atmospheric cycles. Thus, for instance, these admirable fish specially appreciated the last twenty years of relative cold (1960–80). They bore up without numerical damage under the depredations of the fishermen.

The situation today is not so favorable.

4

The Town of Å

Å, in the Lofoten archipelago, is a town that has learned to say thank you.

It expresses thanks first of all for the road. It's a road that comes down from the north and stops there at Å, just after the last house. Past that point, you have to climb, swim or sail: there is no other solution if you want to continue making your way to the south, with its lakes, beaches, sheer rock walls over which eagles fly, its fields of wild whortleberries and its ten or so cabins, more often than not deserted. So all the inhabitants of Å refer to Highway E10 fervently and gratefully. The Government could, after all, have ended the road further north. That would not have made daily life any easier, and would have worked to the advantage of some other town: Sørvågen, for example, or Reine. For the spot where a road ends is bound to attract people. There are heaps of people on this earth who adore end-points. To have approached the extreme limit must make them feel more important, daring, the sort of people accustomed to living on the edge.

Å is perfectly aware that it lives off two things, the second of which is tourism.

Thank you, the town says over and over to the visitor. Thank you for coming all the way here, to us, virtually at the extreme end of the Lofotens.

Å's thank-you expresses itself in smiles, unfailing courtesy, and the size of the dwellings. Why don't you stay in our town a few days, just to take a breather? After close encounters with extremes and limits, a person needs to feel reassured. This being so, Å craftily proposes the use of cabins, cabins that they call "fishermen's huts" but which are in fact dolls' houses. Between the mountains and the sea, Å offers places where you can huddle down. That is the town's second way of saying thank you.

The first way is to sprinkle this expanse of dolls' houses with museums.

A museum has many advantages:

a) It keeps visitors from leaving;
b) It encourages them in their good opinion of themselves:
    b1) if this town has a museum, that must mean it's an important place. "Your instinct has proven to be sound yet again," the visitor says to himself. "You were right to come here";
    b2) if I'm taking a vacation anyway, why not get a bit of culture while I'm at it?; variation on b2) Of course, Norway is first and foremost a lesson in Geography, but that doesn't mean we should overlook her History.

A less intelligent town would have founded just a single museum. Å has created a whole chain of them.

Leading to a further series of advantages.

a) Walking along from one to the next, smiling at the people whose paths she (or he) crosses, losing her way and finding it again, little by little the visitor unconsciously starts to fit in. Soon she (he) becomes a citizen of Å;

b) Fitting in is all the easier because the museums bear names taken from daily life (*the Bakery*, *the Stable*, *the Forge*, etc.) and are scarcely larger than the cabin where the visitor will later spend the night.

Only two of the museums are of more imposing dimensions: *the Manor*, a huge Swiss-style chalet where the town elders customarily met in days gone by, and the *Dried Fish Museum*, which is really the supreme thank you, for if there were no cod, there would be no Å.

There would be no Lofoten either and possibly no Norway. Men have been settled on these rather uncomfortable shores these past 10,000 years for one reason only: they came to fish for cod.

The cod choose January-February, that is, night,

to come here and reproduce. (Out of modesty?) There is no industrial fishing, just small family boats setting out to gather the heaven-sent harvest, in areas clearly delineated by marks traced on the mountains: nets to the north, lines to the south … or the reverse.

And every day the boats come back with their holds full.

To earn pocket money, the youngsters cut out the tongues of the cod. The rest of the family lay the catch out on long trestles and abandon it to the vagaries of wind, sun and rain. As with wine, certain years are better than others.

The Italians, it appears, are the best customers for dried fish, but also the most demanding. They are not to be trifled with. Hence the crucial role of the sorter. He can tell the fourteen grades from one another at a glance. Eight of them for northern Italy (Ragno, Westre Magno 60/80, grade A large, Westre Piccolo, …) and six for southern Italy (Brema, Hollender, Westre Ancona, …). He distributes them among wooden crates beautifully stamped in black ink.

Africa is too poor to afford anything better than

Jakes

155

the fish heads. Å exports tons of them to Nigeria. We are told that these skulls, when boiled for a long period and spiced with hot pepper, are much appreciated by the African peoples and are believed to provide them with an important nutritional supplement.

This Dried Fish Museum, *the only one of its kind in the world* (Tel. 76 09 12 11), is a model both of learning and of near-filial piety.

Everything directly or remotely connected with the dear old codfish is displayed here, and what is more, lovingly displayed: dozens of nets, thousands of fish-hooks, but also scales for weighing cod, the stone for crushing cod, the coating machine for preserving cod, etc. And we must not fail to mention *King Cod*. This fish has a high-domed forehead. Every fisherman had one, nailed up on a wall of his hut. From the changing shapes of the moisture stains left on the wood by this corpse, they could tell what the weather was going to be like.

The museum floor is shaky and of unfinished wood. This gives a double feeling of walking on the deck of a ship and at the same time on the bottom of the sea, for, slowly turning just above our heads, are sinister yellowish mobiles, consisting of ... codfish of every size, hung by fishing line from the very low ceiling.

Good for you, Å!

I have nothing but praise for this affable, intelligent tourism, this tribute to the sea creature that nourishes in so many ways.

You sense, in the air of Å, a wisdom born of direct, thousand-year-old contact with the elements, a peaceful, painstaking philosophy, the fruit of long, unhurried reflection.

But I am a man with an obsession, and so must beg to express one cause for regret. In all its expressions of thanks Å overlooks the Gulf Stream. If not for the current, there would be no clash of warm waters with cold, no eddies to act as purveyors of food, thence no fish and no human presence here. Å would be nothing but some rocks, invisible rocks, moreover, because they would be covered by meters of ice (remember that this pleasant archipelago is located *north* of the Arctic Circle!).

The Ancients were not so scornful of geography. They had named the south-west part of the Lofoten Islands *Vargfot*, that is, "tidal currents at the foot of the mountain."

5

A Strategic Hiding-place

Brest. A December evening. Rain is falling on this city within the city: the Arsenal.

I have an appointment with Vice-Admiral Pierre-François Forissier. He commands "undersea forces and the strategic ocean force."

To reach him, I have to be checked by security several times and walk through increasingly armored doors, the last of which – the door to his office – is so thick and has such a collection of dials to control the mechanism for opening it, that the security staff at Fort Knox, if someone paid for them to come and see, would surely be green with envy.

I have always been strongly in favor of nuclear deterrence. During my three years at the Élysée, I thought constantly about the bunker beneath the

French presidential palace, where the irrevocable decision for a nuclear strike might one day be made. The proliferation of weapons will no doubt change the rules of the game, but don't you agree that the tortuously sophisticated balance of terror is what has given us decades of nuclear peace?

And here I was, in one of the operational sanctuaries of the good witch Deterrence. That thought gave me pause before I asked my obsessive little question:

"How do your submarines use the currents?"

The admiral began his explanation with a bit of ancient history, the history of the stormy relations between the Strait of Gibraltar and those brilliant sailors, the earliest explorers of them all, the Phoenicians.

The Mediterranean is a deep, almost completely land-locked lake. The Suez Canal would not be put through until several thousand years later. Moreover, between Gibraltar and Tangiers the depth of water under a boat's keel diminished sharply. There, a strong west wind blew. The result was a violent surface current bringing waters from the Atlantic into the Mediterranean.

For a navigator curious about the wide world and therefore wishing to go exploring beyond Gibraltar, the task was doubly difficult. His boat was not good at tacking close to the wind, and yet he was faced with two unfavorable forces at once: the breeze and the current. What was he to do?

That was when Phoenician genius made its appearance.

The navigators of Phoenicia noticed a strange phenomenon. When they were in the Strait and paid out a long cable, the cable would at first take its direction from the adverse current: it would drift behind the boat, toward the east. But as the cable sank deeper, it began to hang vertically. And soon, amazingly, it started to point westward, floating *ahead of* the boat.

There was only one possible explanation: under the surface current ran a deep current flowing the opposite way (from east to west).

The Phoenicians were quick to take advantage of their discovery. They invented what might be called "current parachutes." They tied bags of stones to the end of a long rope. In that way, towed by the deep current, they contrived to escape from the gilded but all too familiar cage of their Mediterranean. Discoveries were about to begin.

What the Phoenicians could not hope to guess at was the cause of that subsurface current. It's a matter of salt. As a result of evaporation, the waters of the Mediterranean are very salty, hence very heavy. They tend naturally to sink down into the Atlantic, whose waters, not being as salty, are lighter. And what the Mediterranean loses in water volume at lower depths, it will recover at surface level thanks to the west wind.

End of digression.

⌐

Outdoors, rain continued to fall over the Arsenal. Almost regretfully, the Admiral came back to today's submarines. Their great game of ocean hide-and-seek simply follows the rules first drafted by our Phoenician ancestors.

～

A French submarine is permanently on the move in the Atlantic. In its belly it carries nuclear missiles. The submarine can be spoken to; it can receive commands. These could include pressing the fateful button. But the sub never answers. The only exception to this rule is a situation in which the life of a crew member is in danger. For that reason the ship's doctor maintains a particularly vital relationship with the commanding officer, a relationship that, as mission follows mission, often becomes the foundation of a durable friendship.

The French submarine has departed from Brest for a seventy-day tour of duty.

Is it making for the North Pole, the far southern seas, or is it going to travel along the Equator?

No one knows where it is.

Not even the Admiral.

Each commander is master of his own itinerary. He has been ordered to "disperse." So he disperses.

The submariner is at once hunter and hunted.

Needless to say, he hates this two-way situation; he wants to detect without being detected.

Since darkness reigns in the ocean depths, he hunts by sound. Ears take the place of eyes. Aboard the submarine, the person on the alert for sounds is called *oreille d'or*, golden-ear. How well sound waves travel depends on the water temperature. There are "sound channels" where everything can be heard. There are "shadow zones" where you can lurk without fear of detection. The more complex the water system becomes, the more the skilled hunter enjoys himself and the inept one trembles in his boots.

Why? Because the task of choosing a good hideaway and still keeping the submarine's listening capacity will also become more and more complex.

Legend has it that Soviet nuclear submarines took advantage of the whirlpools to move very close to American coasts without being discovered. For once, reality goes legend one better. To settle into a strategic spot, submarines use all the variables of the sea environment and not just the whirlpools or better-known currents. Like meteorologists, except that their preoccupation is the water not the air, they spend their time analyzing the dance of cold fronts and warm fronts. From their findings they deduce what their course will be.

When they return to port, their tour is carefully scrutinized by the experts. Successes are acknowledged; errors (that is, bad decisions leading to dangerously vulnerable situations) are entered in a *bêtisier*, a register of stupid moves.

Over the years (the first mission goes back to 1972), incalculable quantities of data have been stored up. This knowledge of the ocean's inmost workings is precious treasure indeed, a strategic secret to be jealously guarded, as may well be imagined.

But it is a treasure that can be turned against its possessor. If it leads to systematizing the choices made by submarine commanders, sooner or later an enemy will figure out the logic behind the system.

For that reason the top brass try desperately to break down anything that smacks of routine.

Deterrence depends on the discomfort, mental as well as physical, of the submariners.

꿈

What was that dark, hulking object, over in one corner of the Arsenal?

With a lump in my throat, I recognized the *Bugaled Breiz*, the trawler from Lactudy that sank off the coast of Cornwall, taking with it five sailors.

It was raised, and towed here to Brest. The stem of the ship has two hollows, starboard side and port side, as though a gigantic jaw had bitten into it. There in the darkness I studied, one after the other, the dozens of little round yellow and black stickers pasted to her hull: pieces of evidence. Will they one day reveal the secret of what happened that terrible day?

A long broken line, in which rust is already forming, runs from one side to the other, at cabin level. What force could have bent such a vessel in that way?

6

The Committee on Drift

Sometimes, across the surface of the aquarium, darkness spreads. A special sort of darkness, that will last for days. Darkness that makes everything sticky, darkness blacker yet than all other kinds of darkness. A darkness that does not come from the sky, but – no need to seek further – from a tanker disembowelled somewhere nearby.

This darkness is an oil slick.

Part of it will evaporate. Another part will sink. The rest, the greater part, will gorge itself on water. The darkness will be dispersed in chocolate-colored pellets. The crumbs of darkness start off on their slimy journey. What coastlines will they soil? It is up to the committee to supply an answer. A very special committee, the committee on drift.

Summoned by Cèdre – French acronym of the Center for Documentation, Research and Experiment on Accidental Pollution of Waters – the committee brings together all the government branches concerned.

Hour by hour, calculations are made, using complex models based on a simple formula: take 100 per cent of the speed of the current. Add 3 per cent of the wind speed. You will then have the drift.

The wind is relatively simple: we know where it is blowing from and, more or less, where it will be blowing from in twenty-four hours. But what about the current? There we are dealing with a much more complex beast and one not nearly as well understood, indeed the closer we get to shore the less we understand.

Thus, for instance, the oil that had spilled from the *Erika* was on its way to sullying the Île d'Yeu. A drastic change of wind direction made the slick veer to the north-east. In that quarter, first to be affected were the beaches of the Loire-Atlantique département, after a journey whose direction no one could have predicted: seaboard currents have not yielded up a tenth of their secrets, especially around estuaries.

What form is pollution apt to take in the future? What are the chances of polluted water regenerating? Cèdre studies these additional questions in a strange machine called the polludrome. The machine's mission is to take oil and *age* it. In how many months or years will the sea overcome the oil?

7

A Reservoir of Dreams

Boats and fishes are not the only ones to get carried away by the Gulf Stream. Human dreams, too, are swept out to sea, even if someone soon loses his senses in the process.

One fine day in the 1960s, a big manufacturer turned up at Woods Hole, clamoring loudly for a meeting with the director of the Institute. He was granted an audience.

We have created a perfume that is having trouble making a name for itself in Europe. Here's my plan. I rent a tanker. I fill it with my perfume. I pour the perfume into the sea off the Florida coast. I want it to reach the coasts of Great Britain in time for Easter. Since you people are experts, I expect you to provide me with an exact date. Allowing for the speed of the current, when precisely should I carry out my operation?

～

There is a sort of man that has opinions about everything, notably on how to go about winning a war. With every outbreak of hostilities, not a day goes by but military headquarters receive brilliant suggestions, results guaranteed. Thus in 1942, someone suggested building an immense dam across the Grand Banks of Newfoundland. That would divert the current south, which would have the effect of freezing Europe, starting with the German enemy.

If we take into consideration the greenhouse effect, this engineer, who at the time was held up to ridicule, may have been a visionary.

～

Another dream on a scale worthy of the Pharaohs, this one prompted by common sense: why allow the

171

fabulous power of the current to go unused? Let us erect huge turbines in the Straits of Florida. They will produce more electricity than hundreds of nuclear power plants. And, so as not to harm any passing whales, all we have to do is make sure the giant rotors revolve quite slowly.

∽

Except for a few tidal power stations, little use has been made of the sea as a source of energy up to the present time. With the gradual depletion of oil resources, we will probably be forced to make up for this neglect.

The Gulf Stream is not only a force but also a *variance*. This variance (in temperature) between the current's warm waters and the rest of the sea with its colder waters, is what some individuals – and they are not being foolish – propose to exploit.

The idea of using the ocean's *thermal* energy may go back to Jules Verne and his endlessly inspiring *Twenty Thousand Leagues Under the Sea* (1869). Twelve years later, the savant d'Arsonval put Verne's idea on a scientific footing.

It remained to be seen what would happen when the concept was tested experimentally.

The engineer Georges Claude took up the challenge. An experiment in France, on the banks of the Meuse, convinced him. A foundry was discharging water at a temperature above 33°C into the relatively cold (12°C) river. Using refined circuitry, the engineer produced sixty kilowatts out of this difference in temperature. Then he went away. On his yacht *Jamaica*, he criss-crossed the Caribbean, hunting for the right location. Early in the year 1928, he discovered it in Matanzas Bay, near Cuba. He raised the necessary capital. Working with sections twenty-two meters in length, he soon assembled a wide (two-meter diameter), long (two kilometers) pipe.

Alas, a storm blew up. Half the pipeline was lost. But Claude was not the sort of man to be easily discouraged. There was another fund-raising campaign, then another assembling of pipe-lengths, and another towing. A certain sandbank proved impossible to circumvent. The giant pipe broke and sank. Another failure. The financial backers pulled out. Claude decided to step into the breach with his own money.

The third try was the one that worked. The temperature discrepancy between the water pumped up from the depths and the surface water was 14°C. The little heating plant began to operate.

In Claude's mind, this was just the beginning: the enterprise could now assume serious proportions. He at once proposed construction in Santiago of a fully-fledged power station, with a guaranteed minimum power of twenty-five megawatts. It would be the first step toward making Jules Verne's dream a reality: humanity would have all its energy requirements supplied by the sea. The engineer's enthusiasm would come to naught. Neither governments nor banks showed any desire to become involved. The Second World War put a final end to the venture.

Three-quarters of a century after the "battle" of Matanzas, Georges Claude's unshakeable beliefs continue to gain ground. Not very quickly, for that ground is still strewn with obstacles, notably the foolish belief that oil resources will always be there; this being so, why look elsewhere? The ground being gained is located all over the globe: in Hawaii, in Japan and Polynesia, in California and Taiwan, floating or land-based units are at the planning stage ...

While the hydrocarbon orgy continues unabated, the great maritime projects go quietly on.[18]

V

Dialoguing with the Sky

"[…] the Mexican Gulf and Caribbean Sea are the caldrons; the Gulf Stream is the conducting pipe."

Matthew Fontaine Maury

1

Central Heating

The facts are there, intriguing and stubborn: at the same latitudes, Canadian winters are much colder than their European counterparts.

What can explain this discrepancy – anywhere from 15 to 20°C – of which every passing year brings fresh evidence?

Maury had the answer.

'Modern ingenuity has suggested a
beautiful mode of warming houses in
winter. It is done by means of hot water.
The furnace and the caldron are sometimes
placed at a distance from the apartments to
be warmed. It is so at the [U.S. National]
Observatory. In this case, pipes are used to

conduct the heated water from the caldron under the superintendent's dwelling over into one of the basement rooms of the Observatory, a distance of 100 feet. [...]

[...] Now, to compare small thing with great, we have, in the warm waters which are confined in the Gulf of Mexico, just such a heating apparatus for Great Britain, the North Atlantic, and Western Europe.

[...] The furnace is the torrid zone; the Mexican Gulf and Caribbean Sea are the caldrons; the Gulf Stream is the conducting pipe. From the Grand Banks of Newfoundland to the shores of Europe is the basement – the hot-air chamber – in which this pipe is flared out so as to present a large cooling surface. Here the circulation of the atmosphere is arranged by nature; and it is such that the warmth thus conveyed into this warm-air chamber of mid-ocean is taken up by the genial west winds, and dispensed, in the most benign manner, throughout Great Britain and the west of Europe.

[...]

Every west wind that blows crosses the stream on its way to Europe, and carries with it a portion of this heat to temper there the northern winds of winter. It is the influence of this stream upon climate that makes Erin the "Emerald Isle of the Sea," and that clothes the shores of Albion in evergreen robes; while in the same latitude, on this side, the coasts of Labrador are fast bound in fetters of ice. In a valuable paper on currents (*American Journal of Science,* XIV, 293), Mr. Redfield states, that in 1831 the harbour of St. John's, Newfoundland, was closed with ice as late as the month of June; yet who ever heard of the port of Liverpool, on the other side, though 2° farther north, being closed with ice, even in the dead of winter?'[19]

Born in 1806 in the State of Virginia, Maury joined the Navy when he was nineteen. For ten years and more, he would sail the world over, always off on a voyage. One of his first articles, written in 1831 when he was only twenty-five, deals with the particular problems of sailing in the region of Cape Horn. In 1839, a serious stagecoach accident completely changed his life. His right leg was crushed. He never fully recovered the use of it. He had to give up going to sea. He would continue to study the sea, but thenceforth from land. He was put in charge of the Naval Observatory and Hydrographical Office. In that position he began to bring together all the data on winds and currents available at the time, publishing them as *Explanations and Sailing Directions*, intended for the use of sailors. There, as well, he drew out of the data a synthesis that would constitute his most important book.

The halfway point in the 19th century marks the separation of two eras. The days of sailing ships were coming to an end and so was the poetic near-accuracy of their observations.

Twenty years later, the expedition of the steamship *Challenger* (1872–6) would lay the foundation of modern oceanographic exploration. She had been a sail-powered Royal Navy corvette. She had been stripped of her guns and fitted with a 1,200-horsepower engine to speed her on her way but also to help with the winching and deep-level dragging. The work she accomplished would not pose any challenge to Maury's contentions about the climate of the North Atlantic.

2

A Happy Consequence of Central Heating: The Scottish Rhododendron Society

Nothing, at first sight, could be less welcoming than the vicinity of Poolewe, in the northwest of Scotland: wind, rain, rocks, and poor, acid soil. Also a latitude – 57°8' N – not very apt to conjure up visions of a mild climate (Canada's Hudson's Bay, famous for its ice fields, is located at the same latitude. So are the stretches of country, sometimes icy cold, sometimes torridly hot, in Moscow's far northern reaches ...).

Nevertheless, it was there in Poolewe, that in 1863 a twenty-year-old lord "and sportsman" named Osgood Mackenzie decided he would plant a garden. Until his death in 1922, he devoted to the garden project all his energies and all his means: these latter were considerable, as he was a very big landowner, with 890 hectares, over 2,000 acres. For sixty years, he built: walls, notably, to provide shelter from violent gusts of wind. He levelled and he dug: paths, semblances of roads. And he planted, unceasingly he planted: every imaginable species, provided it came from the British Empire. No setback was spared him: landslides, floods, storms, electrical power failures lasting for months ... He never gave up. One of his daughters, Mairi, picked up the torch. Today the National Trust for Scotland oversees his masterpiece, one of the richest, most varied botanical collections in the world: Inverewe.

It is as though Mackenzie had set out to reassemble a mini-British Commonwealth on his domain. It makes you wonder if he had a premonitory sense of the coming decolonization. With those perennially restless natives, one can never be sure about the morrow; best to bring all the treasures of those lands home to Britain before the heavens fall. A little further down, in Argyll, Scotland, the gardens of Arduaine follow the same botanico-imperial logic.

The results are such that the beholder is – in the

literal sense – transported. From the blue poppies of Tibet (*Meconopsis betonicifolia*) to the eucalyptus of Tasmania, from the lilies of the Nile to the *Olearia* of South Africa, visitors are given a tour of the Empire.

But chiefly the place of honor at Inverewe goes to rhododendrons. In France, these shrubs do not receive the affection they deserve. All that most people remember is small bushes timidly banked together along the edge of a wood, and embellished with a few blossoms that soon wither – not, admittedly, a very riveting sight.

I have to confess that I could be numbered in the ranks of these disdainful folk until the day I found myself marvelling at the blue-tinted bursts of *Augustinii*, the fragile pink-edged whites of *Sutchuenense*, the peacock finery of *Lovinsky* ... And when evening had fallen, what could be more enjoyable, as you sip your Clynelish scotch in front of a peat fire, than to play the delightful game of classification? The sub-genus rhododendron, from the Greek 'rose-tree,' numbers a goodly thousand species, an unmatched playing-field for taxonomy buffs.

Another pastime afforded by rhododendrons is travel tales, for the birthplace of this old, very old plant is the south slope of the Himalayas and western China, regions well above sea level (up to 6,000 meters), all of them vulnerable to the monsoon rainfalls.

Rhododendron hunters were intrepid explorers. Let us give names to a few heros of this conquest, starting with George Forrest (1873–1932), a Scot from Falkirk, discoverer of eight species and varieties. He died of a coronary during an expedition to the heart of Yunnan. Let us salute as well Frank Kingdom Ward (1885–1958): his stories of adventures in remote mountain lands challenge those of Alexandra David-Neel. Nor must we forget the precursors, in most cases monks, Jesuits or Lazarites. All honor to Père David, the man who explored Moupine, on the outermost borders of Szechwan! Honor and Glory to Father Soulié, zealously travelling up and down the Tibet-Yunnan frontier till the day in 1905 when he was shot by rebels ... [20]

And let us all express our gratitude once again

to the Gulf Stream and its North-Atlantic drift! If today we in Europe can enjoy these botanical children of the Himalayas, it is thanks to the mild climate (whose temperature never drops below −10°C and never rises above 28°C) brought to us by the current and its drift.

An Unfortunate Consequence of Central Heating: Mental Illness

The Gulf Stream rouses passions in the human breast. It is a well-known fact that in a person stricken with this disease, the imagination becomes inflamed. The heart is congested with reasons that the faculty of reason finds unrecognizable. The following is a prime example of psycho-climatico-oceanographic lunacy:

'The Gulf Stream transforms that part
of the coast of Europe bordering on the
Atlantic into a temperate greenhouse
[…] The radiation and irregularity of the
current's moist breath are the factors that
combine to give the European his extreme
sensibility and his restlessness, along with

his creative fever and the wonderfully exuberant richness of his civilization. Nowhere in the world can there be found, as there can here, this type of dissatisfied individual, feeding daily upon the climatic stimulation I describe, and seemingly ready at any moment to go beserk. [...]

Were it not for the Gulf Stream and its humid breath, the primitive civilization of the Stone Age with its lapidary art would surely never have existed, any more than those engravings left by the reindeer hunters on the cave walls. And the migrations of ancient tribes would be as difficult to explain as those we have been enduring since 1933.

Neither the Eddic poems nor *Hermann und Dorothea* would ever have seen the light of day; nor would the ministers of the monkish manuscripts of Saint-Gall, nor Rembrandt's paintings; there would have been no Mystics, no Spiritists, no Viking

ships or ocean-liners, no Voltaire or Queen
Victoria, no Paracelsus or Bircher-Benner,
no Luther or Rudolf Steiner, no Columbus
or Auguste Piccard, neither a Karl Marx
nor a Karl May, no witch's broom or
Treaty of Versailles, neither the cathedral
of Cologne nor the Reich Chancellery, no
world wars or UNESCO.

Nor yet would the world possess the
skyscrapers of Manhattan, the hotels in
Bombay, Hong Kong's hospitals, the golf
courses of New Zealand, the plantations at
Dakar, the miniature church of Kuklulu
out in the bush, the New Orleans art club,
the Argentinian railroads, the transmission
pylons in China, the cyclotrons of the
U.S.S.R.

Hollywood's studios, the facilities
at Woods Hole and Tanglewood, none
of that would exist, any more than
the institutions in Weimar, Salzburg
and Geneva. We would never have

> experienced pleasures as disparate as
> Bach's Brandenburg concerto and the
> programs we watch on television.'[21]

The author of the foregoing was called Hans Leip. Was this the Hans Leip who wrote the words to "Lili Marlene," or just someone with the same name?

Despite my research, I know nothing about him, other than the fact that he writes in a town called Wangen, overlooking the Lake of Constance. Leaning out, one should be able to catch a glimpse of the River Rhine, at the exact location where, still a mere child, it resumes its journey up to the North Sea.

Tranquil though this view may be, the soul of our infatuated writer is not at peace. His lyrical outpourings never falter, eventually covering 400 pages.

Pursuing his delirium, he reaches disturbing conclusions:

> Manfred Curry, a German-born American
> doctor, who did research on the effects

of atmospheric pressure, discovered after many experiments the characteristics of two groups of white-race *Homo sapiens*.

[...] They display – a daring contention indeed – the same characteristics as ocean currents. They live in contact with each other and mingle as do the warm and cold currents of the North Atlantic; like those currents, they are constantly in motion, one group seeking heat, the other cold.

Curry has classified them by their reaction to atmospheric pressure – based on their greater sensitivity to heat than to cold or the inverse – into type W (*warm*) and type K (*kalt*).

[...] If, for instance, we consider the characteristics of Norwegian mariners, we find among them prime examples of type W people, stocky, broad-faced, the corners of their lips turned up, eyes set level with their facial skin, their moods shifting in a recurrent cycle, fearful of heat, preferring winter and cold […].

Then there is the other type, type K, represented by those gaunt, hollow-eyed creatures with thin, tight nostrils, less inclined to seek out wind, the type scattered more broadly over the continent and among other European-based peoples. This type includes the descendants of those "shameful sailors" who dreamed of southern warmth and who, working their way down the coasts in successive stages, finally arrived in the sunny Mediterranean regions where heat was not, as in their countries of origin, an occasional and unnatural affair, but rather a permanent atmospheric condition that pleasantly caressed their long-nosed faces and their sceptic's lips that drooped at the corners.'

Someone should write a sort of geography of the mind, with human types and events arranged in an orderly way according to bioclimatic tables. The tension curves of nations should be displayed on the same graph as the scales of dynamic variation found in the Atlantic, in particular those of the Gulf Stream. It might be discovered that these scales of variation mirror the circuit followed by the ocean current via Murmansk and Suez and that they connect up that circuit in a great spiral to all the European centers of turbulent activity.

In that event one might consider comparing the calm zone of the North Atlantic – the Sargasso Sea – to Switzerland, and calling it (based on the experiments of the last 150 years) the barometer of Europe.

4

The Changing Moods of Climate

Faced with recent droughts, floods, storms and heatwaves, some of our contemporaries are amazed to discover that climate is a living thing and that consequently it can *vary* from one era to the next. Worse still, there are others who simply refuse to believe it: for them, such fantasies – deluges, glaciations – belong to remote, barbaric times. According to them, man, having now mastered nature, has presumably mastered nature's little whims as well …

Such people would be well advised to read Emmanuel Le Roy Ladurie and his followers, historians who remind us that nothing has ever been stable or permanent, nothing can ever be taken for granted, especially anything that comes from the heavens.

Since the early 1950s, the University of Arizona

has regularly published its *Tree-Ring Bulletin*, which is sure to fascinate anyone interested in weather.

This journal publishes studies done by a very special breed of scientists: "dendro-climatologists," in other words those who try to unlock the secrets of climates past by studying trees. The principle involved is quite simple: any cut tree-trunk displays a series of concentric circles (the *rings* we hear so much about) that can be counted in order to determine the tree's age. And each of these rings tells a story: it tells what the weather was like in the year that particular ring was formed. If the weather was good, the ring is generous and wide. If the opposite is true, all you see is a thin line.

By observing the characteristics of successive rings, specialists can trace the evolution of a climate, over a period of time limited only by the tree's life span. That is why the sequoia, which lives a thousand years, is considered the ultimate "history tree."

But our good old oak tree can also supply precious information. There is actually one study covering the years 820 to 1964 ...

It is possible, for instance, to ascertain that the year 1473 was particularly hot and dry: the ring pertaining to that year contains almost no water. It is as hard as iron.

⌣

These "botanist-historians" are supported by the practitioners of *phenology*, the science that studies the *dates* of vegetation. They might, to take an example, collect as much information as possible about the blossoming of cherry trees or how early the seasons changed. Let us hear what Emmanuel Le Roy Ladurie has to say. The following lines draw a fine portrait of human curiosity, by which I mean *the wilful desire to know.*

'I, too, set out to discover series of dates
for the grape harvest, from before 1750 or
1800. I located quite a large number of
them in proceedings of municipal councils,
church financial records, police and court
archives of the 17th and 18th centuries.

[...] This "hunt" culminated in a major find: in 1959, thanks to the mysterious god who guides researchers, I was able to lay my hands on *the* key set of documents, on the unexpected treasure that every historian, in whatever specialty, finds perhaps two or three times in the course of a career. At Avignon's Musée Calvet, I literally stumbled upon the huge heap of wine-harvest dates that an efficient scholar named Hyacinthe Chobaut had collected.'[22]

So it comes about that those who know how to read the secrets inscribed in trees and grapevines can tell us about the summers of our ancestors, including certain cruel droughts that shrivelled the cereal crops, giving rise to many a famine; summers that saw river levels drop, creating conditions for infected waters that cause outbreaks of dysentery as murderous as the famines (450,000 deaths in 1719).

❧

Cold has a history as well.

From the end of the 16th century to the middle of the 19th, houses past counting were encircled and crushed by ice. "The glaciers are exploding," as a countryman from the hamlet of Le Tour wrote in September of 1852.[23]

> 'The Argentière glacier has exploded [
> …]. And throughout these last days, the
> Lognan glaciers have been exploding. And
> I, the person writing this, found myself
> at Le Lognan to officiate in the allocating
> of cheeses, and we were obliged to go and
> take shelter in the cellar [of the chalet].
> There was a fearful noise round about, as
> though all the glaciers were falling down
> upon us … From the hamlet of Les Praz all
> the way to Les Tines, the entire highroad
> was washed away by the waters from the
> glacier of Les Bois.'

The *great tide of ice*, which is described here at its

apogee, began around 1590. In the course of those two-and-a-half centuries, it was to mark time now and then, recede occasionally, but continue rising. The "Little Ice Age." Europe was dying of cold, hence starving to death as well. This was true notably in England and France during the winter of 1693–4. Three years later, Finland would experience even worse hardship: one-third of the population died of cold and hunger ...

Since 1850, the glacial tide has been ebbing – which is another way of saying that the Earth is warming. With each new season, the average temperature has climbed a little. It peaked in the mid-20th century (with the torrid summers of 1945 and 1947, so favorable for vintage wines), followed by a certain moderating effect (the word used is *cooling*) ten years and twenty years later, the moderation in turn being a prelude to the present warming trend.

What is the scope of these climatic variations?

The most reliable answer comes from plants. All studies done on European pollens give convergent information. Never again, since the *Atlantic optimum* (of 5,000 years ago), have our European temperatures reached those highs. This, despite certain bountiful interludes (the 11th, 12th and 13th centuries, charmingly dubbed the "lesser optimum").

As for the *average* temperature fluctuations recorded over a very long period, they are limited to *a few degrees*.

Historians have drawn the following conclusions:

- Climate never ceases to vary, nor will it ever cease to vary;
- Even a minimal climatic evolution (a one-degree rise in temperature, a rise of a few decimeters in the sea-level) disrupts human life;
- The current warming trend started a long time ago and so far is modest in scope;
- Climate changes could affect our Atlantic periphery and – possibly with more serious consequences – many other regions of the world.

The story told us by historians spans ten centuries; even to contemplate such a span is enough to dizzy our minds.

But climate is as old as the Earth. To understand what climate is truly like and what makes it that way, so as – next step – to explain its playful little whims, we have to go much further back in time.

That is where paleoclimatologists come in. Their task is to read the past, the very distant past; they read it in ocean sediments, notably in the limestone of very small protozoan animals called foraminifers. They also read it in the snows and pollens preserved in the depth of glacial tumuli ... and they read it in corals.

Thus we can follow the endless drama of climate, in which hot spells and cold spells alternate, while our planet, shaped by plate tectonics, gradually assumes the face we are familiar with.

Ice fields cover the two Poles, the North and the South. Our climate will henceforth be determined by them. How can we explain why, from one era to the next, the ice fields spread, shrink, then spread once again?

5

Dancing with the Sun

A bit of celestial mechanics. At first, scientists thought they could find the explanation for these great climatic cycles, starting with the comings and goings of glaciation, by studying volcanos. The explosion of Krakatoa in 1883 had drawn world-wide attention. Such had been its violence that the noise could be heard 4,000 kilometers away. And it was a long time till a tremendous cloud of dust ceased to darken the sky. Scientists have shown that eruptions send small particles hurtling into the stratosphere, particles with the capacity to reflect a part of the Sun's radiation back away from the Earth, which as a result cools down. But no one has succeeded in establishing a clear connection between volcanic activity, the advance of the glaciers, and climate, much less in measuring that connection.

In this same category of true but partial explanations must be included the element of chance, the fall of meteorites, for instance, which has led to major climatic disturbances.

Some other line of inquiry needed to be followed.

Why not study the relationship of the Earth with the Sun?

After all, the Sun is our heating system.

So our various climates must depend in the first instance on the Sun, on our distance relative to that source of heat.

This common-sense approach had been suggested by many men and women of science. But the person who, using complex calculations, would finally verify the hypothesis and provide the long-awaited explanation was a Serbian physicist named Milutin Milankovitch.

Our planet, as it orbits the Sun, performs a real choreography. Instead of accepting with simple grace the star's proffered warmth, see how Mother Earth entices and teases (I've barely started to come closer to you and already I'm moving away), turning round and round and leaning half-way over.

Let us not belittle this dance of the Earth, even if it strikes us as coquettish: we owe our lives to it. Thanks to these mincing ways, our planet maintains a bearable distance between herself and the Sun. Had she moved too close to the star we would have been burnt up. Had she moved too far away, the cold would have prevented our ever being born.

Let us not forget that "climate" comes from the Greek word *klima*, meaning "slope."

Let us further not forget the involvement of the Moon. If not for its friendly influence, Earth's axis of rotation would be chaotic. Were it not for the Moon, our planet would perhaps have met the same fate as Uranus: one frozen face and one torrid face.

In technical terms, the figures of the dance are called by poetic names: *eccentricity*, *precession* and *obliquity*. Take note! To really appreciate this ballet, you need special eyes, profound experience of what it means to be patient, and ... rather splendid longevity. Why? Because those graceful movements are infinitely slow; it takes 100,000 years, for instance, to alter the shape of Earth's elliptical path. There are times when our planet is moving farther away from its source of heat, and other times when it is moving closer. On these movements our climates necessarily depend.

⤙

Much remained to be discovered. The Sun was not the only player in this great drama. In order for the succession of major cold spells and heat waves to be understood, three new characters had to be brought on stage: the Ocean, the Atmosphere and – a separate personage with her own agenda – the Ice.

We must, in passing, pay tribute to the adaptability required of oceanographers, obliged by the nature of their research to shuttle back and forth between dizzying vastness (the space where stars are) and microscopic smallness (foraminifers, single-celled sea animals), between time that almost stands still (those planetary movements unfolding over periods of a half-million years) and the wild frenzy of the currents (several metres per second).

6

Water and its Travels, Ice and its Rhythms

Over the summer, the sun's rays heat the surface of the sea. Wind stirs up the waters and in so doing disperses the warmer water to a depth of some thirty or forty meters. Thus a reserve of heat is built up: this is *seasonal stockpiling*. In winter, the winds blow harder and the sun's rays are not only less abundant but also more slanted, so they give less heat. The ocean surface now cools. Becoming denser, the surface waters sink, while the deep waters, relatively warm, rise. And that is how heat stocked up by the ocean is restored to the atmosphere.

〜

This first cycle combines with the cycle of the ocean

currents. The waters from the Gulf of Mexico, raised to white heat by the tropical sun, are carried by the Gulf Stream toward the north-west of Europe. They are salty waters, for the initial stage of their itinerary took them along the torrid coasts of Louisiana and Florida where they were more than once subjected to major evaporation.

These warm, salty upper-level waters find their way to the Norwegian Sea. There, they are soon cooled as storms stir them up and icy winds swoop in on them from the Pole. Turning cold, and still salty, they are now dense waters, waters that sink.

But the surface waters do not submerge in a uniform manner. Rather, they form columns, you might almost say "chimneys," a kilometre across. Contingent upon tiny variations in temperature and salinity, surface waters will suddenly plunge, and descend at considerable speed toward the ocean floor. The chimneys are not easy to spot, for they move randomly between Labrador, Greenland and Norway.

So it comes about that at very great depths a current is formed, flowing down in a southerly direction.

The great journey continues. Our current passes along the Antarctic to reach the Pacific. After a very, very slow process of diffusion, the particles of water become warmer, hence lighter. They move back up, toward the surface.

The current sets off again, westward now; it crosses the Indian Ocean, is reinforced by the violent Agulhas Current (a continuation of the equatorial current's southern branch), passes the Cape of Good Hope and flows into the Atlantic. Bearing: north. Joyful reunion with the south equatorial current which carries it due west toward – you've guessed it – the Gulf of Mexico and the Gulf Stream.

The immense cycle has been completed. It will have lasted 1,500 years.

Wally Broecker has dubbed this odyssey "the conveyor belt."

The central heating idea surely did not start with Maury. Arago had intuitively sensed something of the kind, before Maury. But whoever is entitled to be called the originator, today that hypothesis stands verified.

The oceans house a network of superimposed pipes (the currents), some carrying cold, the others heat. In its entirety, the network constitutes a tremendous air-conditioning system.

A system which, like any other, can malfunction.

⌒

Let us imagine that, for one reason or another, the Earth's surface temperature goes up. The ice cap shifts. The break-up begins. Entire flocks of icebergs fall away from the ice cap and melt. Remember that icebergs are blocks of fresh water. As they melt, they release water that, containing no salt, is light in weight, hence will remain at surface level. A substantial increase in rainfall (again, fresh water falling into the sea) would have the same effect.

How do you submerge when you are weightless? The subsurface waters have been expecting to be reinforced by more water, in order to continue on their way. When no reinforcements appear, they stop.

This blockage in the conveyor belt upsets all

sorts of things, among others the course of the Gulf Stream. Its upper branch, the "north-Atlantic drift," encounters a barrier consisting of those light-weight waters that stay at surface level because they aren't heavy enough to sink. The warm current arriving from the Gulf of Mexico stops coming, or rather, comes to us in a weakened condition. All of which explains the following paradox: the more our planet warms up, the more Europe's inhabitants will shiver with cold (though it is also true that Europe will be protected from major heat-waves). That is one possible scenario.

Other models, however, suggest that increased evaporation in the tropics might raise the salt content of one of the Gulf Stream's sources and in that way make up for the melting of the Arctic ice fields.

Watch for further developments ...

In the history of our planet, the conveyor belt has had its share of flops.

The "Climap" program has pieced together a picture of ocean circulation during our most recent glacial period (20,000 years ago). The Gulf Stream's loop had lost much of its portliness. The current went much further up north and the conveyor belt's rate of flow was reduced by one-third.

〜

That is why climate, born of the ocean, is born also of ice: it is dependent on changes in the melting process.

Ice has its own logic, which humans must learn to understand. In 1988, the German geologist Hartmut Heinrich took a core sample north of the Azores. In it, he noted six quite distinct layers which he identified as rock fragments carried along by icebergs, then released by them when the icebergs melted. Shortly afterward, other samplings taken at the same latitude, between Newfoundland and the Bay of Biscay, yielded the same results. He could not, he then reasoned, be dealing with isolated occurrences but rather with a very general phenomenon. Heinrich now proposed an explanation that today is generally accepted. Ice caps, especially over the ocean, grow so big that they finally become unstable. The ice caps break up, and thousands of icebergs are dispersed into the sea where they gradually melt, releasing the rocks they were carrying. As a result of this melting, the water becomes less saline, hence lighter. It stops sinking. The conveyor belt, less and less replenished, slows down. For some thousands of years, cold settles in … until the ice cap re-forms. And shatters once again, releasing more rocks, and so on.

These six ice-cycles have been given the name "Heinrich's events." They each lasted from 7,000 to 10,000 years and, along with the Sun and the sea, were a contributing factor in determining the Earth's climate.

Let Heinrich's perceptiveness be suitably extolled.

Which does not imply that all the mysteries have now been cleared up.

⌒

Twelve thousand years ago we were emerging from

our most recent ice age. Never had conditions been more favorable: the conveyor belt was in peak form, there was a maximum annual amount of sunlight …

And suddenly the cold returned, brutal cold lasting 2,000 years. Was there perhaps a sudden influx of fresh water into the North Atlantic, blocking the heat pump?

How can this occurrence be explained?

The most extravagant hypotheses are bandied about.

One such is the melting of the Canadian ice fields. The fresh waters pour into the Gulf of Mexico via the Mississippi and into the North Atlantic via the St. Lawrence. The Gulf Stream accordingly loses its salt and with the salt its ability to submerge.

Other scenarios bring into play the opening-up of the Baltic Sea (till then a lake collecting waters from the glacial melt) or the separating of America from Asia (the Bering Strait disappears beneath the waters).

The scope of these stories coupled with the great nobility of their chief characters cannot fail to stir jealousy in a novelist's heart.

7

Influence of the Great Winds

The mildness of our winters does not depend exclusively on the sea and its little pranks. The sky refuses to sit idly by. It takes a hand in these grand diversions.

Let us, just for the moment, leave our shores and take ourselves to the far side of the Earth.

Here we are, at the Pacific Ocean.

In normal times, atmospheric pressure is higher off the coasts of the two Americas than over the shores of Asia (Japan, Indonesia, Australia). Thus a steady flow of trade winds sweeps across the surface of the great ocean from east to west. Warm water accumulates in the west of the basin. To restore equilibrium, we have, running the length of Peru and Chile, an upward movement of cold waters, rich in nutritive elements.

Suddenly the mechanism gets out of kilter. The pressure rises around Asia and falls near the Galapagos. The trade winds, normally south-west or north-west bound, die down and then stop, soon to be replaced by winds *from* the west. Warm water is driven back toward Latin America, to the despair of fisher-folk, human or avian, as colder, more nourishing waters stop rising to the surface and the fish starve to death. Or, rather, seek other pastures.

This is the anomaly that has been baptized *El Niño*,[24] and its misdeeds quickly spread to the entire Pacific.

Australia and Indonesia begin to suffer under the worst possible droughts while torrential downpours break over the semi-deserts of Peru. And poor Polynesia lives through cyclone upon cyclone, each more violent than any seen before.

El Niño's activities never last longer than a year-and-a-half. Then its little sister Niña takes over. The trade winds from the east begin to blow again, with all the enthusiasm of someone emerging from a long restful sleep. The cold waters return to their rightful place, from Chile to Alaska. All this to the great satisfaction of the fish and of those who hunt them.

∽

And does the Atlantic stay out of harm's way, safe from the dirty tricks of that scamp *Niño*? Given the unity of the atmosphere, some degree of influence would appear to be inevitable. How widespread and recurrent is that influence? Researchers ponder the matter. Some think they can turn to wine for the answer. They compare the good wine years in Chile, Argentina, South Africa and Australia: they note the differences in time elapsed between the good years and from these differences they infer world climate changes.

However that may be, our Atlantic ocean experiences the same kind of alternation as the Pacific.

There are certain years when the gap widens between the high pressures of the Azores anticyclone and the Icelandic low-pressure zone. Violent winds sweep across the Atlantic from west to east. These storms give Europe winter weather that is unstable but wet and mild. At other periods, the pressure around the Azores and the pressure over Iceland come closer to being equal. The winds die down. Our Christmases are then cold but dry.

Scientists are devoting increasing time and attention to the variation shown by this difference in pressures. They call it the North-Atlantic Oscillation, NAO. The oscillation is thought to influence not only the Gulf Stream's rate of flow but also the route it travels.

⌐

A great part of the scientific community was going happily along with the tried-and-true notion of the Gulf Stream as Europe's main central heating source, when Richard Seager and his team from Columbia University in New York published their work.[25]

These iconoclasts begin their demonstration peacefully. Using sound teaching principles, they recall to mind the three phenomena that can be invoked to explain the relative mildness of European winters:

- seasonal stockpiling; in summer, the ocean stores up the heat received from the Sun; it gradually returns this heat over the winter months;
- the Gulf Stream;
- *the great winds* of the atmosphere.

Having restated these principles, Seager sets out to assess the role played by each of the three systems in shaping the distinctive character of Europe's climate.

According to his team of researchers, the most recent measurements lead to a clear conclusion: the atmosphere brings Europe much more warmth than does the ocean. Were it not for these vast movements of air, winter temperatures in the middle latitudes, which is to say our European latitudes, would be (just imagine) 27°C lower than they are now.

Not satisfied with this general finding, Seager now takes on Maury's contention. Does the Gulf Stream really heat Europe? His response is unconditional: we do not owe our mild climes primarily to that ocean current. In the matter of Europe's temperate climate, the current has just a bit part. Its only unquestionable impact is on Scandinavia. The relative warmth of its waters prevents the coasts of northern Norway from being locked in by ice. Across the rest of our old continent, the Gulf Stream's influence is only marginal.

Since the publication of this work and a few others of the same stripe, debate has raged. Gilles Ramstein, director of the Climate and Environmental Sciences Laboratory (CEA/CNRS) and my Argonaut friends do not have a very high opinion of Seager. Surely we cannot relegate the role of the sea to such an inferior status. Surely no model, however sophisticated, can hope to describe in all its complexity the interaction between ocean and atmosphere. Surely neither of them can be isolated from the other when they have always been intimately linked and always will be. You might just as well postulate a planet Earth no longer revolving on its own axis, or leaving the solar system ...

But perhaps all this is beside the point. Mountain ranges, notably the Rockies, which determine the direction of atmospheric flows, are not about to change position. Likewise, there is no reason why seasonal stockpiling followed by elimination of the sea's warmth should suddenly stop. The only uncertain factor is the future of the Gulf Stream's northern branch (the North-Atlantic Drift). Even a slight alteration of its role, secondary though that role may be, could trigger chain reactions that no one can foretell. To leave out the Gulf Stream is to pretend you do not believe in the frailty of climate. And it follows that you are also relieving mankind of all responsibility.

8

Climate, Born of Man

Poor old Gulf Stream: and you thought you were sole master of all our climate!

After the Sun, the ice fields and the winds, now another actor steps forward to take centre stage.

This is no affront to the activities pursued by our ancestors of 5,000 years ago: there is no evidence that any of their industries, back then, may have had the slightest influence on climate. And yet never was Earth, I mean a planet Earth inhabited by creatures one could consider human, hotter than at that period.

Likewise, factory chimneys of the 19th century do not seem to have been numerous enough, nor their emanations thick enough, to explain the retreat of the glaciers.

Only fairly late on, then, does man become an active agent of climate.

The mechanism is simple.

As always in these matters, we have to come back to the Sun.

Out of a hundred units of energy that the Sun sends our way, twenty will directly heat the atmosphere: before their Earthward journey is complete, they are absorbed by water vapours, dust particles, clouds, and the like.

Thirty other units are reflected back out into space:

- reflected by the air, the ozone, clouds and such;
- reflected by Earth's surfaces, which do not all have the same mirroring qualities: the sea reflects 5 per cent of the radiance that strikes its surface, the forest 10 per cent, deserts 35 per cent and ice fields 80 per cent (so it is easy to understand why this last component plays so great a role in general thermic equilibrium).[26]

The remainder, that is to say half of the energy received from the Sun, is absorbed by our planet, which warms up accordingly.

But the Earth does not remain passive.

Earth in its turn radiates, even if the rays it emits are invisible (infrared).

This radiation, as it rises into the sky, encounters a kind of quilt, composed of water vapour, carbon dioxide (CO_2), methane and certain gasses, prettily yclept chlorofluoro-carbons (CFC).

This quilt absorbs the radiation leaving the Earth, a process which heats our atmosphere accordingly: this is the greenhouse effect.

Thus, our planet receives heat in two ways:

– directly, from the sun:
– and indirectly, by return from the gaseous quilt.

The greenhouse effect has a considerable impact on our climates: without it the *average* temperature at the surface of our planet would not exceed

226

−18°C (at the present time it is 15°C).

And the thicker the quilt, the greater the effect. It does seem that during the primary era the Sun took time off to rest: its radiation had weakened. CO_2 came to fill the gap: there was more of it in the air, so it strengthened the quilt, and thus contributed to maintaining temperatures at such a level that periods of glaciation were averted.

If man can do nothing about other climatic factors, he does contribute to the building up of an increasingly thick quilt.

The energy we consume comes from what we burn: oil, gas, coal, wood. All involve the combustion of carbonous elements, generating CO_2.

At the same time, our wholesale destruction of forests releases into the atmosphere the carbon previously retained by the trees.

Then there are those chlorofluorocarbons we were discussing: much used in industry, they, too, contribute to the density of the quilt.

As for methane, which is twenty-one times as active as carbonic gas, its increased presence in the air is due to demography. The two main sources of methane are flooded lands such as ricefields, and animal excrement. The more the world's population increases, the more rice that population requires and the more livestock it raises ... And if the warming trend persists, the permafrost, that permanently frozen land in Earth's cold regions, will soon thaw, releasing the enormous quantity of methane it contains.

As the intergovernmental groups of experts on climate change discreetly concluded in 1995, "a cluster of data points to the likelihood that there exists an appreciable influence of man on climate." Unlike our Gaulish ancestors, we do not have to fear that the sky will fall down upon our heads, but that an unduly thick quilt may be suspended over us.

〜

What kind of greenhouse will our grandchildren live in? A hundred years from now, will the planet we bequeath to them have warmed up by 1.5°C, or by a great deal more?

In their attempt to answer, scientists continually devise models of ever-greater complexity. But how can they include *everything*, take into account *everything*?

Shall I give an example? Consider the way they deal with clouds, those marvellous clouds, as the poet said. Do you realize that there are clouds, and then again there are clouds? Ice clouds that let the Sun's rays through. And water clouds, more opaque, that instead reflect those rays. In the model, what weight should be given to each type of cloud?

Poor Gulf Stream!

During the holidays every year, I would glorify it as being *the* benefactor, the divinity coming from America, to whom I owed the near-tropical exuberance of our Breton gardens and the (relative) balminess of the waters I swam in.

And now my wanderings were revealing a gigantic opera in which the current was just one character among many.

Worse still, they had reduced the size of my Gulf Stream, shrunken it, confined it between the Gulf of Mexico and the middle of the ocean. After that it became the "North Atlantic Drift." This change of name struck me as insulting and, to put it bluntly, idiotic. When I take the train to Brittany, the high-speed section stops at Le Mans. But I'm still aboard my TGV, my high-speed super-train.

Both these injustices plagued me and I could not let the matter rest.

Friendship, unlike love, takes people as it finds them. The fact that someone does not lay *everything* as a gift at your feet does not mean you must stop taking any interest in that person.

You continue to hanker after an *overall* explanation. But partial truths are also worth grasping. And there is this to be said in their favour: they do not stifle you; they leave you your freedom.

As for ocean currents, I did not lose interest in them merely because my beloved Gulf Stream had been called into question. Quite the reverse. My journey had taught me that all currents, whether at sea or on land, have things to tell us: about the nature of pathways and the secret of first beginnings.

VI
Paths in Motion

"Tao can be called the path, the way;
only, it is a path in motion."
Paul Claudel

1

Sitting Outdoors at the Kjelen Café

Norway, high latitude: 67°15'. Thirty-three kilometres past Bodø, along the road to Seines, I
advise you to slow down. On the left-hand side,
between the church and a grey house which will turn
out to be a museum (always closed), a road appears.
Do not on any account miss it. For at the end of it
the Kjelen Café awaits you. A large room filled with
mementos (old fishing-rods, lanterns, photographs of
Narvik in 1905, others from the opening of the café
in 1959), but quite a cheerful room (the chairs are
yellow and red). Take a moment to run your eye over
the menu "Fish Special" hanging from the ceiling
(you have a choice of halibut, cod or Atlantic bass),
then move on to the outdoor seating area. If there
exists a human being who is not overwhelmed by

the spectacle that then greets him (or her), take that person – but at once! – in your arms. And console her (or him), with every sort of consoling caress or strong drink: you must on pain of death reawaken in the sufferer a taste for the world around him and that right speedily.

In the background, mountains. A few peaks, some patches of snow to add dignity. But the whole effect is more like a gam of whales. Grey, rounded shapes, worn, scraped down, a tired skin furrowed with deep wrinkles, the scars of a long life and one that cannot have been easy. Prehistory bears this out: there was a time when one to two kilometres of ice lay heavily over this part of the world. The landscape is recovering, little by little. Freed from that great weight, the land is rising back up; but the after-effects of the massive crushing it endured will stay with it forever.

Lower down in the picture, the countryside, gentle, varied and attractive, considering this land is so close to the Pole: we are further north here than Iceland, almost on a level with Baffin Bay. And yet there are woods, dense ones; fields in soft shades of green; the cows graze among the rocks; and all sorts of delicate flowers are there to greet you (*Aconitium wilsonii* and their blue helmets, *cochlearifoli* campanula and their little white bells, pink carpets of stemless silene, all these and more).

A botanist could spend a profitable hour there, marvelling at the vitality of species that have so few weeks to live before the cold weather returns.

But a dreadful thundering makes it impossible to concentrate on questions of botany. At our feet there flows the world's fastest-moving current, a real Maelström, to console me for my disappointment in the Lofotens: the Saltstraumen.

Around the year 1000, Olav Trygvason, the King of Norway, decided to be done with Viking chief Raud den Rame who was tyrannizing the region. Not only did he pillage, rape and murder, but, quite content with his totally pagan existence, he refused to embrace the Catholic faith.

Olav's navy sailed into the harbour bottleneck.

Raud, who had the forces of nature at his command, unleashed the fearful waters.

The fleet drew back; vessels foundered.

Time out for a war council.

Olav decided to take a holy bishop on board before launching another attack.

Wise move. The Saltstraumen laid down its arms. And so did Raud.

⤚

The Bretons were astonished: how can a dwarf-sized tide – less than two metres in amplitude – unleash such a torrent?

Answer: the narrowness (less than 150 metres) of the bottleneck separating the Skjerstad Fiord from the Salt Fiord, which opens into the sea. This is the needle's eye through which, four times each day, 400 million cubic metres of water has to pass. Whence the violence. At a speed reached nowhere else on Earth: over twenty knots on good days. Plus giant whirlpools (ten metres across and hollowing down as much as five metres at their centre). More than 100 certified drownings; so church records show: the victims' names are inscribed in a black book at the church.

After you have shuddered, as is only right and proper, it is time to celebrate the virtues of the Kjelen Café and its outdoor seating area. Built out above the raging waters at a most advantageous spot, just upstream from the bridge, it affords the most perfect possible viewing point for this phenomenon of nature, a summation of everything I had learned about currents, which comes down to two basic principles.

A current is not really a path or a road: it has no edges. Or rather, its edges constantly escape. First there will be a break-away, which forms a curl, which soon becomes a whirlpool that takes on a life of its own.

A current never comes singly. It is always accompanied by a counter-current, as though to remind it of the basic principle of all life in society: for every power, a counter-power; for every majority, an opposition.

Monday, 9 August.

Suddenly, at about 6 p.m., came the festivities, fast and furious, one after the other with no intervals.

Stimulated by the rising half tide, the Saltstraumen increased the tempo of its dance. The waves, sweeping along, stretching, twisting, turning inside out, were going mad. While the surface was having deeper and deeper whirlpools dug down into it, not far away other waters were making it swell and bloat. You would have thought springs were welling up, springs coming from the fathomless depths and constantly shifting their position.

Apparently this frenzy whetted the appetite of the fish. Below the Kjelen café, the fishermen were going nonstop. Casting, striking, reeling in, unhooking, casting again. The baskets were filling up fast.

Which suited the seagulls just fine. They were lined up on the roof. Every minute or so, they would dive down, nearly grazing the top of our heads, to fight over the entrails of the fish that were being gutted as fast as they were caught.

A little later, a dolphin came to join in the fun.

The children were jumping for joy and shouting every time the dolphin's brown back emerged from the waves. "Over there, in front of the buoy!" "Just in front of the lighthouse!"

And then Norway gave us one last gift. There is a club that brings together those who have seen, seen with their own eyes, as we did that day, a fishing eagle. There are, so people say, 8,000 of these lucky ones; they publish a newsletter and meet occasionally to swap fishing eagle stories.

The great bird was wheeling in slow circles, a sovereign inspecting his domain, master of all he surveyed.

I thought of the photographer Henri Cartier-Bresson. I had learned of his death shortly before setting out on this trip. Some years earlier, we had worked together on a book about his landscape photographs. He would invite me over to his place to give me lessons in looking and seeing. From high up in his lair on the rue de Rivoli, there was a view of the Louvre, the Orsay museum, the Tuileries, the place de la Concorde and other landmarks. We would discuss grammar and geometry.

The afternoon was drawing to a close; the dance of the current gradually subsided, but the light was still the same. It seemed as though the Sun would stay there, suspended forever at the same place in the sky.

High latitudes.

2

Vagabond *on her Way*

Latitudes differ somewhat: this one may read 68°30', that one 55°. To put it another way, the first of these is not as far south of the North Pole as the second one is north of the South Pole.

Tromsø in Norway is so similar to Ushuaia in Argentina. How did the two sisters come to be so distant? What family falling-out led to their separation?

Aside from that, there are only resemblances.

The same mountains, not very high but with patches of snow. The same dark waterways, fiords, straits or canals, now broad, now narrow as though choked off. The same low clouds, the same sensation that at these extreme ends of the planet, earth and sky are going to meet and perhaps crush us all. The same moderate tides, the same nearly-orange seagulls. Inhabitants with the same passion for beer. The same depressingly dirty roadways, the same gravel and potholes. The same feeling that on calm, mild days the city has been orphaned; it has lost both its parental authorities, the cold and the wind.

Vagabond, she of the appropriate name, does not like to sail in a straight line. It takes deep knowledge, or rather foreknowledge, to hold a steady course. If vagabond means wanderer, our ship indeed wanders. She seizes the helmsman's slightest moment of inattention to go see what's over there in some other direction, twenty degrees to port or thirty to starboard. You need to correct *Vagabond* before she even starts taking one of her fancies to veer off. Failure to anticipate her whims carries the penalty of zigzag courses, alas clearly inscribed in the waters of her wake, giving irrefutable proof that the helmsman is a useless twit who deserves – worse than jibes and taunts – the suppressed smiles of the crew.

Thus did *Vagabond* waltz her way up toward the Far North.

Now it was like sailing on a canal. Smooth sea, both motors humming, shorelines parading slowly past. Now and then a red and yellow village huddled around its church. Apart from that, solitary houses, all at the water's edge. No human presence on the slopes; the wind must blow too strongly up there.

We fall into a routine.

In the morning, seamanship, in other words lessons in knot-tying: everybody knows the bowline and the old, reliable capstan knot, but how about the carrick bend, the three fold overhand, the Turk's head, the wall-knot, and this knot, and that one? Tying knots soon becomes an obsession. How can your fascinated gaze not be drawn to the love dance – held right there in your fingers – of the *standing end* (the fixed portion of the rope) and the *running end* (the part that twists and snakes in and around)? How can you not be reminded of certain secret ceremonies at which the Japanese are expert? Using the most sophisticated knots, you tie the one you love, forcing her or him to assume all sorts of positions, or even to hang suspended for a long period of time ...

Lacan, toward the end of his life, lost all interest in everything but knots. Mathematicians would call on him in the Rue de Lille to present their latest théories on the borromean …

At noon, the barometer reading: it's falling.

And in the evening, as soon as pre-dinner drinks have been served, we each of us put forward our individual dream.

Any ship is an ark.

Noah (that is, the captain) has brought together on his vessel, for a few days or a few weeks or whatever time the trip may involve, species that he wants to save from the Flood (I refer to the humdrum of daily life on land). Aboard the *Vagabond* were to be found only specimens of a very particular species of human: the lover of ice. Every kind of ice, sea-ice as well as land, vertical ice as well as horizontal, glaciers as well as ice-floes, all sorts of ice.

Against a background of salsa or samba (musical taste aboard the *Vagabond* tends toward the Caribbean), all I now hear is talk of ice, of scaling ice walls (you would think they were all mountain-climbers, whereas I've never lived in an apartment above the third floor for fear of dizziness), of treks across the ice (Arnaud has crossed the Arctic pulling his own sled), of temperatures braved in order to reach ice-fields (Marc and France have tackled the Drake, the formidable strait separating Latin America from the Antarctic), of pitting one's wits against the ice (what game of hide-and-seek with icebergs could equal Eric's and France's exploit: circling the North Pole in a sailing craft?).

Ice has become the main character on the boat. And from it, as from those seaman's knots, I have something to learn.

Eric Brossier had this tale to tell:

23 August 2001.

Caught in the ice, *Vagabond* lay dozing in the Jensen Fiord, on the coast of Blosseville, east of Greenland. Blue sky over the white expanse, winds calm. No one was paying special attention to that big iceberg over there, to seaward. And anyway, what exactly is "the sea," "the open sea," when it's as frozen as the shore and as a result perfectly motionless? In those hours of utter calm, the Arctic, once discovered, enters your soul and never leaves.

The first sign of anxiety was mutual questioning: Doesn't it strike you that the iceberg over there is getting bigger? No, of course not, don't be silly. Soon, no one had eyes for anything but the iceberg. Yes, it was getting bigger. Which meant it was coming toward us. Listen to those cracking sounds. It's smashing the ice floe. How high is it? At the very least, it rises well above the ship's mast. Thirty metres? Forty? Not to mention the part you can't see, that whole mass below the surface. A mountain was heading toward *Vagabond* where she lay imprisoned in her ice ...

At the last moment, slow-moving as ever, relentless as ever, the iceberg passed us by on our right. Otherwise, we wouldn't be here.

I had never thought about that form of violence on the part of a current, when it takes to using icebergs as battering rams.

〜

Listening as my companions told about their climbing experiences, I began to understand why sea-people and mountain people are alike. What is a mountain, after all, if not a wave permanently set in position? What is navigation, if not horizontal mountain-climbing?

～

Dinner that evening was entirely given over to reminiscences of being adrift at sea. Every one of *Vagabond*'s passengers had at one time or another been carried off by ice. In the tales they had to tell, one name kept recurring: Nansen. Apparently he was revered. I could vaguely remember certain childhood readings, the *Journal de Spirou*, Spirou's Diary, and "Les belles histoires de l'Oncle Paul," Uncle Paul's Very Best Tales. Uncle Paul, pipe in hand, would tell the stories of famous scientists and explorers. Timidly, I asked to have my memory refreshed.

"What? You've never heard of Nansen?"

Speechless, they gazed at me: in their eyes I read a mixture of sympathy and kindly contempt.

The year was 1893. Fridtjof Nansen was thirty-two years old. He was a scholar (doctorate in science) and a sportsman (he had just crossed Greenland on skis). People had always found, along the coast of Canada, pieces of wood and various bits of debris that had come from Siberia. They could only have got there borne by a great east-west current.

Nansen's idea was simple: build a vessel able to withstand the pressure of the ice floes and then let the ice carry him along. That way he'd soon find out whether the North Pole was in fact land or sea. Funding for the project was obtained. On 24 June, the *Fram* set out from Norway with twelve men and thirty-four dogs. On 24 September, arriving at the mouth of the Siberian river Lena, *Fram* was caught in the ice as intended. The drifting began. A slow, monotonous drift that would go on for eighteen months. Aboard the *Fram*, they passed the time as best they could. By the spring of 1895, it was clear that the Pole would not be reached in this manner. The boat was now only at 85° latitude. There were five degrees yet to go. On 14 March, Nansen decided to leave the ship. He took with him just one companion, Johansen, plus a sled, two kayaks and twenty-seven dogs. Three months later, he realized that no more than his ship would he ever reach the Pole. The ice masses were too uneven, fissured with crevasses, and interrupted again and again by stretches of open water. The two men turned back. Their goal was the Franz Josef archipelago, 360 miles to the south-west. After any number of adventures and misadventures, they paddled their way to one of the islands, where they would spend the winter of 1895–6, alone, living as the Eskimo do. With the return of spring, they climbed back into their kayak and put out to sea again. They reached Cape Flora. There, on 17 June, they came upon an English traveller.

"Are you Nansen?"

"That's right."

"I'm very glad to see you."

Nansen, now a national hero, would not be satisfied with this first brilliant feat. He was also responsible for the document that so greatly eased the lives of countless refugees from the Great War, the famous

"Nansen passport." This good deed would earn him the Nobel Peace Prize. Probably he was still obsessed with people who are adrift, and not just among the ice floes.

My friends aboard *Vagabond* fell silent. Quite obviously, Nansen was their hero. It would be hard to fault them for their choice.

Marc, our mountain climber *cum* architect, a specialist in bridges, spoke up again.

"When they were found, the two men looked rather like a pair of savages, but they were in excellent physical shape. Wintering out had agreed with them. And they had each put on ten kilos. Polar bear meat is reported to be tasty and nourishing. Nansen was asked: 'Wasn't it too harsh an experience?'

'It was a pleasant trip'."

⌇

I was destined to meet up with this Nansen, and quite soon.

Basking in the glory of her two "crossings," the

sailing-ship *Vagabond* had become the stuff of legend. On that account, she was given a hero's welcome by maritime museums everywhere.

In Tromsø, a berth of honour was reserved for us, right below the Polar Museum. There was just one drawback: the ladder leading up onto dry land was eaten away by rust. It was safer to climb up using the tires fixed against the dock to act as bumpers. Mere child's play for my mountain-climber buddies. They heaved me up.

And we opened the door to that large edifice of red wood.

Hung on its walls are fox skins, seal skins, reindeer skins and dried bodies of birds. Also to be seen are weapons, all sorts of harpoons, and sculptures done in wood or bone. A trapper's hut has been reconstructed. Inside it you can listen to water boiling on a makeshift stove, stray animals howling, the whistling of wind and the ominous cracking of ice on the move.

Seated behind a desk, Nansen receives visitors on the upper level. He is wearing an evening suit, presumably the one he wore for the Nobel Prize ceremony. But his gaze is permanently fixed on the kayak, *that* kayak. The other reminders of his epic journey seem to interest him not at all.

Before taking your leave, be sure to say hello to Amundsen, his fellow figure of legend. You are not unaware that Amundsen was the first human of all to reach the South Pole. But did you know what a noble death he died? He was trying to rescue an Italian adventurer who had insulted him.[27] Amundsen's (French) aeroplane never came back.

3

Courances, or the
Magic of Fresh Water (I)

Courances, one of the sweetest names our geography has to offer, and one of the most softly rhyming. Courances, fifty kilometres from Paris, one of the most perceptive gardens to be found anywhere; planned, of course, but left in its natural state, that is, fragile, and free from political agenda.

Courances: something is running, as in *courir*, but the essential element remains.

Courances: a running, a flowing, but also a constancy.

"The white purity and the current (the *blancheur* and the *courant*) of the waters in this lovely spot have caused it to be named Courances. Such is the clarity of its waters that at the bottom of their channel the beholder may distinctly observe very fine trout." That is how Dézallier d'Argenville described the place in his *Voyage pittoresque des environs de Paris* (1768). And that is how today's traveller finds Courances to be.

⁓

Once upon a time there was the 16th century. And everywhere, water was finding new employments. With progress in weaponry, moats were no longer of any use: since they no longer protected castles from artillery salvos, why not convert them to ornamental ponds? Water invited itself to the garden party, notably in Courances which swarms with natural wellsprings, fourteen of them, supplemented by Rebais Brook, and the River École (from the Latin *colare*, to flow). Early in the 17th century, the garden took shape, a simple garden, as Pascal Cribier succinctly put it: "Water, grass, stones and trees." Especially water, in its every shape, round, octagonal, rectangular, ... water running or still, level or peacefully flowing down broad steps or shooting furiously up from a little crowd of big-mouthed creatures disguised as dolphins. The variations are endless.

Any park, any pleasure-garden worthy of the name will have a central theme, those visual perspectives that tell your eyes where to look next. You feel carried along, as though bound to follow an unspoken order. Geometry at its core is really a network of currents: the eye follows a line, which is not so very different from a tidal flow. But Courances, unlike Versailles, does not impose upon the visitor any particular itinerary. At Courances there is no Sun King; no Colbert lurking in the shadows; no mythology to be inculcated. The water is content simply to set you in motion. Feeling its presence, whether visible or hidden, hearing it, whether murmuring or thundering, how can you help but feel caught up and carried away? You would swear you had never left solid land and lo! suddenly the whole garden is afloat. And who is to say where a freely drifting, floating garden may fetch up?

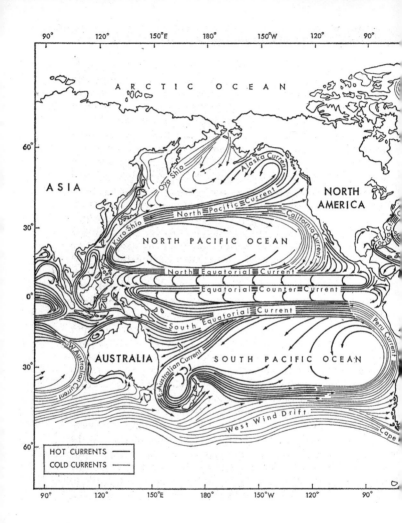

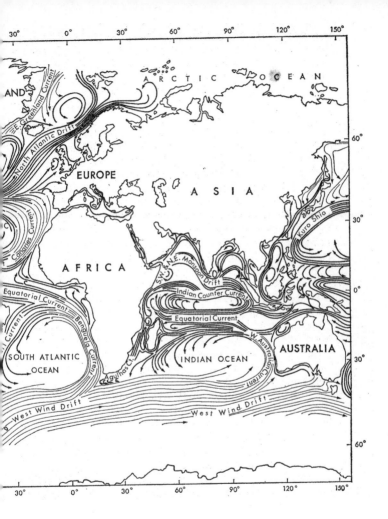

4

The Magic of Fresh Water (II) The Ganges

According to the *Mahabharata* and certain Sanskrit anthologies rediscovered by Jacques Lacarrière,[28] in the first days of the world the Ganges flowed up in the sky. Down below, meanwhile, the Earth was choking, already submerged under the ashes of humans no sooner dead than burned.

The gods deliberated and hit upon the idea of sending the river down to clear our planet of all that unwanted dust.

O, fools! Shiva said to them, you will drown the Earth in a terrible flood. I suggest that the Ganges follow the course of the hair on my head. Winding thus and with its current divided, it will flow by and do no harm.

Shiva stuck out his head. But its tresses were

258

so luxuriant that the waters became lost in among them and wound aimlessly about in that jungle for countless years, vainly seeking an egress.

And all that time, men went on dying, dead bodies went on being burned, ashes continued to accumulate and the planet continued to choke.

At last, after untold centuries of spiritual exercises, the river "spread over the earth amidst shrill cries, while shoals of fish and turtles, troupes of crocodiles and other animals fell or had fallen from the skies to enhance the splendour of the earth. Then the gods, those wise ones, watched the Ganges going down from the firmament onto the earth. Mounted on chariots resembling cities, on horses, elephants and watercraft, the divinities gathered in haste to witness the wondrous descent of the Ganges into our world – gods though they were in their measureless state of being. And while they flocked thus to the scene, in all the lustre of their fine apparel, the cloudless firmament shone forth as though lit by a hundred suns. The troupes of crocodiles and snakes and the darting fish scattered sudden shafts of light everywhere about.

The jets of foam-whitened water filled the air like autumn clouds, along with the serried flights of the flamingoes [...]."[29]

5

Corryvreckan or the Echo of the Tides

My trip to the Isle of Jura (Inner Hebrides) strengthened me in the notion that water is not the only thing moved by ocean currents. Not only in the atmosphere but also on land, far beyond the shore, currents trigger mysterious movements that involve the workings of innumerable forces.

One fine late-autumn day, I had set off for Scotland to pay my respects to a monster: Corryvreckan. A saltwater torrent with a flattering reputation: along with Norway's Saltstraumen and The Old Sow in New Brunswick (Canada), Corryvreckan is said to be one of three most violent floodtides in the world. Sailors bold enough or reckless enough to have ventured into it know for the rest of their days what it means to be truly afraid. Isabelle Autissier, for example,

261

remembers being caught up. Her boat, which, mind you, was sixty feet long, started to behave like a top. It was whirling, faster and faster, as though in the trough of a giant toilet basin. The rudder had ceased to respond.

Rather than describing the spot, Swedish navigator and writer Björn Larsson prefers to quote what the manual of the Clyde Cruising Club has to say about Corryvreckan:

> '[Corryvreckan] is at its most dangerous when an Atlantic swell [...] meets a flood tide. A passage at this time would be unthinkable. [...] In calm weather at sp[ring tides] the first can rise to a height of 4m, and may be accompanied by a loud, roaring noise as it plunges from the Scarba shelf. A heavy w[esterly] swell can double its height, when it and the remaining overfalls drop to the bottom of the deep, and possibly angled, troughs. In extreme conditions the roar can continue for several

hours, audible even at Crinan, 6 miles
distant. [...] Prolonged strong w[esterly]
winds can make an overfall, perhaps better
described as a solid wall of water, stretch
from here, and also from the shelf, right
across the gulf [of Corryvreckan].'[30]

"Deep troughs," "wall of water," "a passage would
be unthinkable" ... Each phrase an irresistible call to
the nature lover.

In short, on my arrival at Oban, it seemed to me I
had reached the approaches to Hell. And in my room,
Room 12 of the good old Alexandra Hotel, I spent the
night reviewing the facts of the case, starting with the
physical data. First, the narrowness of the strait, at that
location the only door open between the Irish Sea and
the Atlantic. Then the slope: from west to east, the
bottom goes down by a good metre. And, jutting up
from that same sea bottom, a single rock, twenty-nine
metres high. Not high enough to break the surface but
all the more formidable for that very reason: the raging
waters twist around the rocks to form the whirlpool.

Legends had no difficulty embroidering further on this wild, fierce reality. In Argyle, people will tell you that a witch lives in the whirlpool. She is the one who decides whether to let a ship through or swallow it up. The very name of the current comes from the Gaelic *Coire*: "cauldron," and *Bhreacain*: "mottled."

But other, more noble origins have been found, such as the account that Hamish Haswell-Smith, tireless explorer of the Scottish isles, enjoys repeating.

There was once a Norwegian prince, one Breacan. Arriving by sea from his native land, like many of his ancestors and cousins, he fell in love with a young lady from Jura. The father of the beautiful maiden decided to put her suitor to the test. "Anchor your boat for three days running in the middle of our strait and my daughter is yours." The prince, sensing a trap, made inquiries among the local sailors. The only way to survive the wrath of the current, they told him, is to attach your anchor to three ropes, one made of wool, the second of hemp, and the third made from hair belonging to the young virgins of the island. You may guess what followed, and also the sad ending. At the end of the first day, the woollen hawser broke. Next day the hempen one parted. Till finally the third and last cable tore apart, dragging to his deep watery grave a fiancé credulous enough to trust the good faith of those islanders. The least they could do was to christen the fatal cauldron Breacan …

﹏

When morning came, I put in an appearance at the tourist office. Feeling intimidated, and speaking softly so as not to rouse the devil's anger, I inquired: against all reasonable expectation, might there possibly be a fisherman bold enough to take me close to the ill-famed current? A young person with round, rosy cheeks laughingly handed me a whole wad of advertising pamphlets: a dozen tour-operators would be glad to show me the whirlpool. Two hours and a half of unforgettable shivers and shudders. Your safety guaranteed in our giant inflatable zodiacs. Twelve pounds for individuals, with reduction for families.

Imagine my disappointment. Here, as every-where else, our planet was apparently becoming an amusement park.

Everest and Cape Horn can thank their bad weather! It's the only thing still protecting them. If not for the weather, if not for its terrible high-altitude or upper-latitude storms, the roof of the world would become nothing more than the next subway station after Kathmandu and the mythical rock merely a good-luck stop on honeymoon trips.

I needed to go about this some other way, use a side entrance approach in order to give magic a second chance. An explorer has to resort to trickery these days if he wants to recapture the freshness of pure geographical pleasure.

And so it came about that, thanks to two ferry-boats, after three hours of road travel and almost as much boat crossing, I finally arrived at Islay. Great was the temptation to stop there and pay my respects to the noblest of "peated" whiskies, Lagavulen and especially Laphroaig (a whisky whose gamut of aromas is a journey in itself, ranging from licorice to iodine).

I ought also to have commemorated the very ancient kingdom of the Gaels. Their masters, who bore the splendid title *Lord of the Isles*, resided here. From the 13th century to the 16th, they had for their entertainment a brilliant court, rich in poets and musicians.

But my appointment was with Jura and only Jura, Jura the neighbouring isle, *Deer Island*, home of the fallow deer.

In its one village (Craighouse), the only hotel is a family affair where you are almost immediately on easy terms with everyone. A single glance was enough to tell grandma-barmaid what was on my mind.

"You don't look like a climber, *you* don't; or a hunter, either. That means you'll have come on account of our Eric."

So an ocean-current fancier does not have a particular kind of face, and can travel incognito. Good to know. But who exactly might this person be, this man with the same first name as mine who was obviously Jura's pride and glory?

The woman in charge realized how uninformed I was. Annoyance flickered in her eyes. A barely perceptible shrug of her broad shoulders accompanied her answer to my inquiry. But her kindly good humour had returned, and with it an indulgent smile.

"That's right, I was forgetting. You French people don't even know his real name! Poor Eric! Why call him George, when his name was Eric?"

And that is how, while I was looking for Corryvreckan, another gift entirely was presented to me, the beautiful, sad story of one of the major novels of the 20th century, *1984*. My hostess broke off time after time to go and serve an increasingly jolly, noisy roomful of customers. The tale she was telling progressed slowly, bit by bit. Later, I would learn that these bumps and jolts were a foretaste of the road leading to George Orwell (rightfully Eric Blair). Each time, in order to get herself started again, she would use the same preliminary phrases: "A quiet sad-looking man" – that was her refrain – "and dogged by ill health … ".

The war had lasted a long time for him, starting back in 1936, in Spain. Nor had 1945 brought him peace. He felt his life being doubly devoured: firstly by London, with various requests to do this or do that plus the fragmenting effect of work as a journalist; and secondly by his tuberculosis, steadily worsening month by month. His wife died. Escape was imperative. One day, Jura saw him arrive, in the Post Office delivery van. With him was his adopted son, Richard, age three. He had found a farm, Barnhill, in the north of the island, 23 miles from here. You'll see, "it's ... remote." *Remote* like some combination of the French *lointain, distant, isolé* ...

&#x21 dc;

The island of Jura gives the impression of a large, sleeping animal. From hump to hollow, you move along the animal's back, slowly so as not to disturb its sleep. The colour of the animal's fur changes, depending on the light and the time of day: from reddish brown and tawny, via every shade of ochre, to faded pink with an assist from the heather. Ahead of you stretches a long string of cows, very reluctant to move off to the side. Why are they so fond of the road?

Now I know the answer: they like to shit on it. But I will need further trips in order to grasp the reason for this preference. From time to time, you walk along or across a village: Lagg (five houses), Inverlussa (seven houses), Lealt (three houses) …

The chief population of Jura is not human. I had stopped to admire Loch Tarbert, when I heard a faint sound. I turned my head. Perhaps three metres behind me was a ten-point stag, firm and motionless upon a hillock. Side by side, we stood for some time enjoying the view, till at last, taking long, unhurried strides, he left me. He was shaking his head in a front to back motion, as though nodding it in approval.

The road becomes more and more difficult to negotiate and then it disappears, changing suddenly to a track, a peat-bog, a pothole. With no horse or 4x4, you have to walk, six miles. *"It's remote."*

Finally, in a glen on my right, with its back well protected from the north and the west and its front looking out over a small bay, there it was: Barnhill.

I had encountered the owner along my way. He opened the sanctuary for me, toured me through the house, and showed me into the holy of holies, a bedroom above the kitchen. This was where Eric had dwelt for the space of two years, sitting up on the bed with his back propped against a pile of pillows. He had his own special way of holding his typewriter pinned between his legs so it couldn't slip. Everyone who visited the house during that period remembers those fierce gusts of sound that never stopped, the furious noise of his typing. Nor have they forgotten the strong smell of tobacco. Orwell, who chain-smoked, was forbidden to open his door; he stank up the whole house. The moisture-rotted ceiling sent big flakes of plaster showering down onto his head.

Now and then, he would tend his kitchen garden. He had planted an ambitious array of vegetables, but his hopes of living self-sufficiently on the meagre output of his tiny domain were quickly dashed. He had a single unwavering obsession: he wanted to muster his strength and rely on that alone.

His sole means of land transport was a motorbike which broke down with great regularity, affording the district much matter for comment. He would gaze helplessly at his motor. *A quiet, sad-looking man* ... One of these days, they all repeated, he'll have to give in and take a course in mechanics.

Sometimes, probably seeking even greater solitude (after all, the working title of the book that became *1984* was *The Last Man in Europe*), he would make his way to the west side of Jura by the only possible route: water. No road, not even a path leads to that precipitous line of cliffs pitted with caves and patches of beach. You can picnic there with no other companions than puffins and seals.

And that is when "my" Corryvreckan reappears.

One day, Eric forgot the rules; he took his boat out at mid-tide, the time of greatest turbulence. The whirlpools caught him. The waves swamped his motor. The boat capsized. Richard disappeared. Eric dove in, managed to grab the child. Huddled on a rock, father and son would have a long wait before a boat came to their rescue.

I can imagine that the spirit of the waters, this Corryvreckan, must have hesitated before handing down a judgment on the fate of the foolhardy pair. I like to think it was curiosity that moved the spirit to show clemency. Ever since I visited Jura and was told this story, I have considered Corryvreckan the perfect example of a literary, politically aware ocean current. How else can we explain its benevolent decision? If it had not wished to know how *1984* worked out, would it have saved the book's author who was currently hard at work on his novel?

～

From Barnhill to the northern tip of Jura is a good two hours on foot. Naturally, the traveller guides his footsteps to coincide with Orwell's, along a narrow winding path, just barely a track over the heath. Nothing has changed in half a century and most likely in thousands of years. No buildings. Still the same moorland under foot and, up in the sky, the same slow circling of those eagles that gradually take the place of sea birds as you approach the shore. Where did Eric used to stop? Did he have his favourite rock, the way Ernest Renan had his favourite chair, a granite chair on the island of Bréhat, overlooked by the lighthouse and the signal-post?

Across the strait, the isle of Scarba is nothing but a cliff. It's as though the Creator had only done a general outline of the isle: it never completely emerges from the mist.

And down below, the current, blue, grey, green, depending on the day and the wind, occasionally black, always streaked with foam.

You can understand its violence by looking west and not finding anything, no coastline, nothing but untrammelled sea. Consult the map. Ireland doesn't start till further down and Barra, the most southerly of the Outer Hebrides, is anchored more to the north. So it is here, into this bottleneck, that the ocean plunges on its arrival from America. And through this same channel it will leave again, six hours later.

Of course we can never get inside a dead man's thoughts except by breaking and entering. And there is every likelihood that we will guess wrong. What thoughts passed through Orwell's mind as he faced Corryvreckan? We can reasonably suspect that they

274

were not cheerful. What did the current tell him that he did not already know? There he was, a veteran of the Spanish Civil War, with first-hand experience of Fascism and Communism. What could fill him with greater despair than the spectacle of this alternating violence? Violence unleashing its fury from right to left, with all the heart and cruelty at its disposal. Six hours later, the violence changes direction. The same determination and comparable cruelty, only this time the raging waters are coming from the left. How can a man believe in Action and Progress when faced with the daily spectacle of the tide? Anyone who claps his hands for the rising tide is deliberately forgetting that the water is going to go out again. In this strait between Jura and Scarba, Life is what is putting on a show, Life with its ungovernable pulse and its cycle.

6

The Songlines

On land as well, an attentive observer will detect innumerable "paths on the move." I do not refer to landslides, cave-ins, collapses, I do not refer to *natural events*, nor to the grand interplay of the continents and tectonic plates. It goes without saying that our planet is constantly in motion. And its movements, sometimes terrifying, bear witness to the vitality of the globe. But the only movements that interest me here are the itineraries, the actual routes followed ... by *currents*.

China is the country that has mapped out this phenomenon most fully.

Geomancy (from the Greek *gē*, "earth" and *manteia*, "divination") is called in China *feng shui*, that is, "wind and water." To capture the breathing of the mountains, to situate the happy marriage of the elements so that the living and the dead can inhabit the earth in harmony, surely these are goals to which anyone can subscribe.

In the beginning is the vital breath, *qi*. The object is to identify the most propitious locations on the planet, those places where the vital breath has concentrated most favourably.

> 'If the breath rides the wind, it is
> dispersed. If it meets water, it stops. The
> Ancients did not allow the breath to
> disperse if it accumulated and held it in
> check if it circulated. That is why the art
> is called wind and water. The procedure in
> feng shui consists first of finding the water,
> then of holding back the wind.'[31]

Feng shui is not merely a philosophy, an esoteric discourse on the hidden principles governing the world. It is a system of practices. No matter that it draws on an art of arrangement so intricate as to make your head spin (the five agents with their two cycles of begetting and domination, the ten celestial trunks, the twelve earthly branches, the sixty-four hexagrams, the eight trigrams ...); its applications are extremely concrete. The person who can make a drawing showing what course the breath follows, and where it lodges, will also be the one who can recommend to the builder the right place for putting up his house, or to the gravedigger the appropriate spot for digging a grave that his dead client will enjoy.

'It is important to know that there exist within the Earth's crust two magnetic currents, if I may so express myself, one male, the other female, one positive, the other negative, one favourable, the other unfavourable. The first is called allegorically the Azure Dragon, the other the White Tiger. The Azure Dragon must always be on the left and the White Tiger on the right of the place that is assumed to be a favourable location. Hence the first concern of a geomancer in search of a favourable place is to find a true Dragon and its complementary White Tiger, both of which he will recognize from certain rises in the terrain. The Dragon and the Tiger are always compared to the upper and lower parts of a man's arm; you must find the favourable spot in the bend of the arm. To put it another way, the site that holds out the promise of happiness, the location for a tomb or a dwelling, these may be found in the angle formed by the Dragon and the Tiger, at the exact point where the two currents represented by them intersect.'[32]

In such a conception of the world, man is not different from nature: "magnetic currents," the kind that acupuncturists call "energy," run through humans as well. We shall leave it to others to describe these needle games, but not without recommending to our readers a practitioner in the ninth arrondissement of

Paris, not far from a department store specializing in fashions and "youthful design." The office of this pica-dor-doctor is worth a visit, if only for its waiting-room. There, secretaries reign, never the same ones you saw before, but always dark-haired, smiling, and with skin so white it takes your breath away, and conveying an indefinable aura of open-mindedness, as though they were prepared to set off on certain kinds of journey, provided only that these take them to far-away places and be culturally enriching. The patients, and patient they need be, spend hours there in the waiting room, for the master of the house cultivates tardiness as though it were the essential curative plant. No voice is raised in protest. You settle back into the softness of the wicker couch (which creaks). You keep your voice down. You savour the green tea made by the young lady. You pick an (oriental) book from one of the three bookcases. You let yourself be lulled by Bach, never anything but Bach, his German or Italian ritornellos, which, mingling with the incense vapours, transport you to somewhere east of the Indus. When the doctor finally emerges, hand outstretched and smiling broadly, my-dear-friend-how-are-you, a strange feeling of well-being has already taken care of you.

Later, much later, when you are back out on the street surrounded by the regiments of prostitutes (had you already inferred that this was a red-light district?), wonder of wonders, they're smiling at you, as if to say: "Well, here's one man at least who got what he came for. Anybody wearing such an unmistakable look of satisfaction is a walking advertisement for our trade." You thank them with a polite nod of the head; and as you watch the hesitant approaches of their customers, the walking by and coming back, the circular paths of desire, there is doubt in your mind. Will the lovely ladies be able to calm human fever as effectively as the picador?

This area of the city has always struck me as fiercely maritime: there are so many people going by that they lose their individuality and begin to blend, soon forming a crowd, and the crowd circulates like water. Two rivers with turbulent waves, the rue Mogador and the Chaussée-d'Antin, empty into the sea, the boulevard Haussmann.

Whenever my longing for Brittany is too great to bear, I go to this confluence to enjoy the spectacle, if possible on a Saturday in mid-December, at the height of the shopping frenzies, those storms of Advent. From up above (you merely have to go a few storeys up and open a window), it looks like the tidal currents off the Île de Sein, or like the Fromveur: the same furious rising or ebbing tides, the same timid countercurrents of window-shoppers. And the same whirlpools: you would swear that they are suddenly breaking away from the main flow to take on a life of their own. Indifferent twice over, these breakaway whirlpools: indifferent to the general press and haste of the crowd (some of them whirl slowly) and to this mania for completing the course (they revolve endlessly on their own axis).

❧

Man can influence the circulation of the vital breath. He is not doomed to passive acceptance. By making appropriate changes to what was basically an unfavourable site, he can "find the water and hold back the wind." This gives you some idea of how important landscaping is in Asia, and what keen attention will certainly be paid to the course and direction of that self-same breath by anyone putting in a garden, a miniature landscape.

To this basic *feng shui* couple must be added the "mountain," real or imitation, always the point where energy builds up. The mountain, *chan* and *shansui*, is the landscape … And the rocks, called upon in so many cases to play the role of mountains, are immersed for years before any use is made of them, so that the water streaming past has a chance to mold them. The most highly prized stones are believed to come from Lake Tai Hu, west of Shanghai. They probably possess special erosion characteristics.

As to the passion of the Chinese for water, it has always impelled them to sail the seas, of course, but in their own particular way: without moving. At the end of the 19th century, their government had voted funds to modernize the navy. Empress Cixi misappropriated these moneys to restore the old "Garden of Pure Waters." And, since a navy, after all, must have a ship, she had one built: a replica in stone of a Mississippi paddle-wheeler!

In the "Garden of Harmonious Interests," one can walk across the "Bridge for the Understanding of Fish." People of culture spent hours in contemplation of the carp, trying to imagine what was passing through the minds of those dumb creatures[33] ...

How far removed this is from the Gulf Stream!, schoolmasters will exclaim as they relentlessly hunt down anything "not on the topic." Let us respect their concerns but carry on regardless.

The rover insists on his inalienable rights, in this case the right to address you on the topics of doors, an unlucky politician, handwriting and Australia, in that order, before rejoining the Atlantic motherhouse.

While a certain number of *feng shui* rules come under the heading of common sense and a practical mentality (best possible exposure to the sun, good use of the prevailing winds to try and cool the torrid summers, etc.), the jungle of other prescriptive usages is virtually impenetrable to the Western mind. We had best confine ourselves to a single example, the shape and placing of doors. In a Chinese garden, the visitor may be astonished: why is it always so inconvenient to move from one place to another? Why have they deliberately made it so? Why are there such zigzags, why these circular doors (moon doors), these narrow bridges, these galleries that suddenly bend at right angles? The answer is strategic: it is advisable to prevent evil spirits from invading this space. And since evil spirits move from one place to another only in a straight line, …

The uncontested prize for the most tortuous pathway goes to a park in Suzhou: the famous "Garden of the Unlucky Politician." Wang Xianchen lived in the 16th century. His career as a senior civil servant had brought him nothing but troubles. Like many of his lettered colleagues whose ambitions had not been fulfilled, he had bought a piece of land and cultivated a garden, a Candide-like form of exile as old as

China. The walkways in this garden would turn you giddy. If the proprietor took such elaborate precautions, it must have been because he considered the evil demons of politics particulary sly …

↬

And lo, the sheet of paper becomes the whole world. And the breath is made stroke of the pen. Listening to François Cheng is a great privilege, a privilege apt to turn into an addiction. The psychoanalyst Jacques Lacan, we are told, would question Cheng to the point of exhaustion. Mister Cheng, what is China? Night would fall over number 5 rue de Lille, the dark becoming inky, deep and black. The head of this most learned Chinese man would droop forward with fatigue, his slanting eyes would close and Lacan went on asking questions.

Now it is my turn: I take up Cheng's books, read him with passionate interest and torment him with questions. How can anyone not marvel at the idea of a Creation permanently in motion? It would appear that we are the infinitesimal agents of *becoming*, a prospect that must surely delight people of activist temperament. When Cheng begins to quote Heidegger: "*Being* is that which never ceases to change," it is as though the Earth suddenly shrinks, just enough to fit onto the square of paper.

Then the echoes become sonorous, the allegory vertiginous; as for the breath, why, that's the current, of course. And handwriting, calligraphy? The ultimate stage in cartography.

> '*Not rejecting*
> *stones, the mountain*
> *remains high;*
> *Not turning back*
> *the waters, the ocean*
> *becomes vast.*'

(Guanzi)

〰

But China does not have a monopoly on non-ocean

currents. In *The Songlines*, Bruce Chatwin tells the story of Arkady Volchok, the son of Russian emigrants who had settled in Australia. After brilliant results in his university studies, he suddenly frustrated his parents' wishes by deciding not only to become a schoolmaster, but to volunteer for a teaching appointment in a remote spot north of Alice Springs.

There he gradually came to know and appreciate the Aborigines. From them he discovered the existence of the labyrinth, an intricate network of invisible paths covering all of Australia.

What were these paths? They were the paths of Creation. In the Dreamtime, totemic creatures had criss-crossed the continent and "by singing the names of everything that they had encountered along their way – birds, animals, plants, rocks, water holes – they had brought the world into existence." These paths are not shown on any map; how, then, are we to rediscover them?

By doing what those Creatures did, that is to say, by singing. That is why these legendary and endlessly repeated itineraries are called the *songlines* or "dream tracks," or "ancestral footprints" or "lawful paths."

The Russian had won the confidence of the Aborigines. They took him along on their walkabout-poems. He, in exchange, drew up for them an official register of the labyrinth. A very odd legal document, but one that would help them, in a way, to preserve their sacred sites from the greed of promotors, developers and the like.

I met Chatwin once, on the rue des Saints-Pères in the very heart of Paris. I was petrified by the special sort of shyness that admiration can trigger. It took all my courage to accost him. Many things puzzled me, especially this: why had so notable a nomad halted his journey when he was in South America? Having reached southern Patagonia, why had he not pushed on south? Why his total silence about Tierra del Fuego? Why had his insatiable curiosity not taken him further down, past the Beagle Canal to the island of Navarino? And further down yet, beyond Nassau Bay, to the Wollaston archipelago? Why no visit to Cape Horn? Did the legends of the sea not interest him?

He looked at me uncomprehendingly.

Only later did I understand the surprise in his blue-eyed gaze.

It was when I read *Songlines*.

The sea definitely does not have exclusive rights to invisible yet vital routes of travel.

Silk Road, Amber Road, Tea Road, Opium Road, Salt Roads, trans-Saharan camel routes, there is no end.

All these are "paths that move forward," everywhere across the planet; all are lines of force, as the physicists say, calling to human beings and guiding them; all are land-based currents.

In the words of wanderer *par excellence* Nicolas Bouvier, anyone not aware of these terrestrial currents can never claim "to be making good use of the world."

Epilogues

1

What is an Oceanographer?

What is an oceanographer? Speaking of his friend Arago, Alexander von Humboldt said that he had "a natural disposition for considering, in their mutual connections, a great number of objects at once."

2

Bottles into the Sea
(continued)

I asked my friends in the Argonaut Club: "This book owes you so much; are there any messages you would like to send out, using the book as an opportunity?"

They put their heads togethers and debated at great length. If I'm not entirely misinformed, there may even have been a wee bit of shouting and table-pounding.

Here are the three bottles they are entrusting to the sea:

1. In the great story of weather, the sea plays the main role. So, combining their efforts, the nations of the world must, as quickly as possible, create an international observatory of oceans and climates.

2. The ocean receives from the Sun an amount of energy one thousand times greater than our requirements. Let us exploit the sea's thermal energy.

3. Let us make use of what we learned from the Asian tsunami (26 December 2004). Beginning at primary school, let us learn how to observe the sky, sea, land, rivers, animals … let us learn how to observe nature.

   And many lives will be saved.

3

Flotsam Seaweed

February 4, 1953. Blue sky over the western tip of Europe, winds light, glassy sea. Jean Le Gall has just put out from Camaret. He is twenty-three years old. The world is his, for he is at the helm of his first boat, the *André*.

His life is just beginning.

Tomorrow and every day, through all the years to come, he will fish. On Molène island, his wife Marianne (age twenty-two) sees him coming in. She has a little girl in her arms and another child is trotting along beside her: three-year-old Jean-Yves. She goes back into the house for a moment; a few last touches are needed for the special meal to celebrate the boat. She steps back outside, but now there is nothing to be seen. The ocean is an empty expanse.

The *André* has struck a rock called Chevreuil. Only one of the three sailors will be saved.

⮌

Fifty years later.

A Tuesday in December. A stiff norwester breeze, thirty or thirty-five knots, sea already heavy. Is it really wise to take a Parisian on board for a trip through the islands?

"He's a writer."

"What's that got to do with it?"

"He collects currents."

"So?"

"He wants to see Fromver."

"Too risky."

The warden of Molène nature reserve is very reluctant. Louis Brigand is a geographer, a specialist in coastlines and, incidentally, one of the commissioners of this very reserve, but it takes all his diplomacy and obstinacy to win consent for the expedition and have his Parisian allowed to board the dinghy.

Our boat is under way.

What between spindrift and yawing, the warden gradually relaxes. Relaxes, opens up, and starts to talk about himself. Later on, I will realize that he knows all there is to know about birds, fish, crabs, lobsters. But his first story is the one I just told you, that boat disaster one February day. He is that child, that orphan, little Jean-Yves, today a grown man. Can you understand now why he gave us such a rough reception? I can.

That day we would not go as far as Fromver (too risky). We stopped at Banneg Island, which lies along the eastern side of that raging current. If perchance you should venture one day into those boulder-infested waters, would you allow me to offer a word of advice? See to it that you always "keep Kéréon lighthouse between the two rabbit's-ears." Appearances to the contrary notwithstanding, this utterance is not a magic incantation. Nor is it, carried by the wind, a last message from "This is London calling; Frenchmen are speaking to Frenchmen."[34] It's simply a recipe to help you avoid wrecking your boat, a gift of geometry, called *alignment*.

It must be admitted that we were pretty scared. None of the people on board had forgotten that on a boat the word "rabbit" has always and forever brought bad luck.

Perhaps to reassure me, my two friends had undertaken to inform me about stormy petrels.

"They love Banneg Island."

"Banneg is where they nest."

"Did you know they were the smallest of all the sea birds?"

"Just barely over twenty grams."

"They winter in South Africa."

"And you wouldn't believe how smelly they are!"

"They're also called *sataniques*, devil-birds."

"Because they nest in burrows."

I wasn't giving these precious bits of information all the attention they might have deserved, for on our port side the water had gone from being troubled to being seriously angry. The ebb tide was rushing violently through the gap between a jumble of rocks and the northern point of the island. The retreating sea, furious at being suddenly hemmed in, was smashing, forming hollows, rearing up; it bellowed, and spat white foam.

"You wanted to see Fromver, did you? Well, this is it. If anything, a calmer than average day: neap tide and moderate winds ... " I took out my note pad, gripping it in numbed fingers, and jotted down the name of this nightmare: Versit Hole.

"I can also recommend, in this group of islands, ... "

And that is how my collection of currents grew to include Chimère Channel, to the south-east of Molène, and Mogol Islet. Thrills and shivers guaranteed.

Jean-Yves looked at me.

"Why are you so keen on currents?"

"That's a long story."

"D'you know where they found my father?"

" ... "

"Three week later, up against the Pointe du Raz. Opposite Sein, the island where he was born. Naturally."

"Naturally."

⌒

What is a *pigoulier*?

A fisherman farmer; I mean, a person who gathers seaweed.

There used to be thousands of them, up and down the coasts of Brittany.

If you will excuse this quick summary, there are two kinds of algae, or seaweed. The kind that is cut at low tide, to be used as fertilizer or fuel. And the other kind, much more highly prized, flotsam seaweed, those long brown strips that the currents tear loose from the ocean floor and cast up on the shore. There was a time, not that long ago, when the gatherers spread the flotsam seaweed out on the moors to dry. Then it was burned, slowly, in rectangular ovens hollowed out into the earth. What was retrieved from the ovens was something resembling black stones, loaves of soda, which factories on the mainland transformed into iodine. Progress

301

in chemistry and the advent of antibiotics effectively wiped out the *pigouliers*.

We had a bite to eat in one of their shelters. There is nothing like cold, semi-darkness and ruins to take you back in time.

My two companions were probably angry with the Atlantic for shaking them around and soaking them to the skin that morning. And also for stealing fathers from a good number of kids. They began to discuss a very distant era when salt water was not so arrogant.

"Did you know that 4,000 years ago the sea was much lower than it is today, so low that the mainland jutted out all the way to Fromver channel? At that time Molène was not an archipelago but the modest summit in an area of hills where people simply came to hunt."

"Look!"

On the ridge of a big rock facing due south were hollowed-out cupules, perhaps ten very small, perfectly even holes.

"What happened here, on that rock? What were our ancestors playing at? Greeting the sun?"

No matter that the wind had strengthened and the waves begun to roar; one and all, we had stopped paying them the slightest heed. Indeed their turbulence almost struck us as over-the-top, theatrical.

I had come to this place to witness the ocean's mighty anger, and instead found myself in the muffled mists of prehistory and its enigmas. I had come to explore one of the noisiest outposts in space, only to be greeted by time, the almost unspeaking time of first origins.

The journey is never the journey you expect.

That the horizon should elude our gaze, well and good; it is in the very nature of horizons to flee.

What really scoffs at us and scorns us is the *destination*. The paths we follow always take us someplace other. There are those who will react to this ungovernable behaviour with annoyance and frustration. The rest know deep down in their souls that the ungovernable behaviour is another name for the spice of life.

Thank-you's

More than any of my other books, this "portrait" owes a debt to friendship.

And to the generosity of experts.

Thank-you to Nathalie Daniault and Alain Colin de Verdière (University of West Brittany), my first professors of oceanography.

Thank-you to that tremendous assemblage of expertise from many fields, the Argonauts Club, and thank-you to each of its individual members: François Barlier, Michel Gauthier, José Gonella, Jean-Paul Guinard, Jean Labrousse, Michel Lefebvre, Jacques Merle, Michel Petit, Bruno Voituriez, Raymond and Madeleine Zaharia.

Thank-you to Claude Allègre. Among his other recognized qualities is his unmatched ability to tell people about science.

Thank-you to Brigitte Millet, who opened for my benefit the doors to Ifremer,[35] that temple of oceanographic exploration.

Thank-you to Herlé Mercier (also of Ifremer). To him I owe my (few) notions of fluid physics.

Thank-you to Louis Brigand and Jean-Yves Le Gall, respectively commissioner and warden of the Molène archipelago nature reserve.

Thank-you to the women scientists at Legos (Midi-Pyrénées Observatory, Toulouse). I apologize, but the only people I met there were ladies: Frédérique Rémy and Catherine Jeandel. I ought also to have paid my respects to the great Anny Cazenave; unfortunately she was away on assignment.

Thank-you to Admirals Méret and Forissier, notable personalities in the French Navy.

Thank-you to the team of Océanopolis in Brest, starting with the director, Éric Hussenot.

Thank-you to Camille Lecat, tireless nomadic oceanographer.

Thank-you to "the pope's son," Phil Richardson. I shall never forget how welcoming he was to me at Woods Hole (Massachusetts).

Thank-you to France Pinczon du Sel and Éric Brossier for accepting my presence aboard *Vagabond*, their already mythically legendary sailing ship.

Thank-you to Gérard d'Aboville. More than any other sailor, the person rowing a boat is aware how treacherous currents can be.

A double thank-you to the people at Cèdre (*Centre de documentation, de recherche et d'expérimentation sur les pollutions industrielles*) for the information they provided me with, and for their unremitting fight against the sticky, black horror of oil slicks.

Thank-you to Nicole Momzikoff. She, too, has a boat, but hers is Parisian and if it does not appear to move, that is merely illusory. On the fourth floor of the *Institut océanographique* at 195 rue Saint-Jacques, the library that she runs with warm, friendly efficiency can transport the user to the edge of the visible world and well beyond.

Thank-you to Isabelle Autissier, who gave me access to her catalogue of the most violent patches of water on our planet.

Thank-you to Hervé Hamon, who regularly meets Force-12 winds in the Ouessant region, and who has so eloquently written of his need for the sea, his *Besoin de mer*. His many foolish impulses include believing in this foolish project of mine, to which he contributed, day in and day out, unflagging support.

And thank-you to Charlotte Brossier, the good fairy who copes with impossible manuscripts.

Thank you all.

Were it not for you, I would still be sitting at a table in one or other of the bars I patronize, dreaming about a book that would finally convey my love for the sea.

Bibliography

To date (3 January 2005), the search engine Google, that irreplaceable ally of inquiring minds, has compiled 1,610,000 references to the Gulf Stream.

Which gives some idea of the interest – and the controversy – stimulated by this current of ours. I shall limit myself to the essential.

Allègre, Claude, *Introduction à une histoire naturelle,* Fayard, Paris 2001.
— , *Histoire de la Terre*, Fayard, Paris 2004.
Bard, Édouard, *Évolution du climat et de l'océan,* Collège de France-Fayard, Paris 2003.
Carpine-Lancre, Jacqueline, *Albert Ier prince de Monaco*, Monaco, EGC publishers, 1998.

Cazenave, Anny and Kurt Feigl, *Formes et mouvements de la Terre*, Belin/CNRS publishers, Paris 1994.

Cazenave, Anny and Didier Massonnet, *La Terre vue de l'espace*, Belin, [series] "Pour la science," Paris 2004.

Chapel, A., M. Fieux, G. Jacques, J.-M. Jacques, K. Laval, M. Legrand and H. Le Treut, *Océans et Atmosphère*, Hachette, Paris 1996.

Duplessy, Jean-Claude, *Quand l'océan se fâche, histoire naturelle du climat*, Odile Jacob, Paris 1996.

Fellous, Jean-Louis, *Avis de tempêtes*, Odile Jacob, Paris 2003.

Hemingway, Ernest, *Îles à la dérive*, Gallimard, Paris 1971.

—, *Le Vieil Homme et la mer*, Gallimard, Paris 1952.

Joussaume, Sylvie, *Climat d'hier à demain*, CNRS publishers, Paris 1999.

Larsson, Björn, *La Sagesse de la mer*, Grasset, Paris 2000.

Le Roy Ladurie, Emmanuel, *Histoire du climat depuis l'an mil*, Flammarion, Paris 1967.

—, *Histoire humaine et comparée du climat, canicules et glaciers, XIIIe-XVIIIe siècles*, Fayard, Paris 2004.

Maury, Matthew Fontaine, *The Physical Geography of the Sea and its meteorology*, New York 1855; French translation, *Géographie physique de la mer*, Librairie militaire, maritime et polytechnique, Paris 1861.

Minster, Jean-François, *La Machine océan*, Flammarion, Paris 1997.

Morel, Pierre and Jean-Claude Duplessy, *Gros Temps sur la planète*, Odile Jacob, Paris 1990.

Rémy, Frédérique, *L'Antarctique. La mémoire de la Terre vue de l'espace*, CNRS publishers, Paris 2003.

Stommel, Henry, *The Gulf Stream. A physical and dynamical description*, University of California Press, Berkeley 1965.

Stowe, Keith, *Exploring Ocean Science*, John Wiley & Sons, New York 1996.

Sverdrup, Harald Urik, Martin W. Johnson and Richard H. Fleming, *The Oceans: Their Physics, chemistry and general biology*, Prentice Hall, New York 1942.

Thurman, Harold V., *Essentials of Oceanography*,
    Macmillan, New York 1993.

Vanney, Jean-René, *Introduction à la géographie de
    l'océan*, Institut océanographique, Paris 1991.

Voituriez, Bruno, *Les Humeurs de l'océan*, Unesco,
    Paris 2003.

—, *Le Gulf Stream*, book in preparation for Unesco.[36]

— and Guy Jacques, *El Niño*, Unesco, Paris 1999.

Ocean Circulation, Open University/Pergamon Press,
    Oxford 1989.

La Recherche, "La Mer," ultra-rich special issue,
    February 2003.

Not to mention the published work of the
Argonauts, whose website is a mine of information:
www.clubdesargonautes.org

Notes

1. For, like all other lands, Norway rests on fluid matter.
2. Plato, *Phaedo*, translated by Hugh Tredennick; in *Plato, The Collected Dialogues including the Letters,* ed. by Edith Hamilton and Huntington Cairns. Princeton University Press, 1994, Bollingen Series LXXI, pp. 92–93.
3. Paulus Merula, *Cosmographiae generalis libri tres*, Amstelodami: 1605, p. 171, and Adamus Bremensis, *De situ Daniæ*, Lugd. Batav., 1590, pp. 247–249. Quoted by Albert the First of Monaco on the occasion of his presenting to the *Académie des Sciences* the results of his oceanographic expeditions (1890).

4. Athanasii Kircheri, *Mundus subterraneus*, liber III, p.160. Quoted by Albert the First of Monaco, *ibid.*

5. See Pierre Grimal, *Dictionnaire de la mythologie grecque,* PUF, Paris 1985.

6. T.S. Eliot, *The Dry Salvages.* In *Poésie*, bilingual edition, Seuil, Paris 1947.

7. M.F. Maury, *The Physical Geography of the Sea,* (new edition, Sampson Low, Son, & Co., London 1856) pp. 321–2. Courtesy of Mills Memorial Library at McMaster University, Canada.

8. Henry Stommel, *The Gulf Stream: A physical and dynamical description.* University of California Press, Berkeley 1965.

9. Henry Stommel, *Lost Islands: The Story of Islands that have Vanished from Nautical Charts,* University of British Columbia Press, Vancouver 1984.

10. Which I do not recommend to anyone. But the other inns round about look no more inviting than mine.

11. S. Ferraroli, J.-Y. Georges, P. Gaspar, and Y. Le Maho, "Endangered Species: Where Leatherback Turtles Meet Fisheries." *Nature*, 3 June 2004.

12. Respectively, *Météo-France*, the *Centre national de la recherche scientifique*, the *Service océanographique de la marine*, *Ifremer*, the *Institut pour la recherche et le développement* and the *Centre national d'études spatiales*.

13. My thanks to Bruno Frachon, hydrographic engineer. I am indebted to him for all this information about Arago.

14. In my case, the road to this club went by way of Africa! One day, a reader wrote to me. He had read with interest my novel *Madame Bâ*. I wrote back. We met. His name is Raymond Zaharia. He is a physicist and an engineer. He spoke to me at once about his special interest: observation satellites, and about his mentor in the field, Michel Lefebvre, a man with a thousand ideas per minute. I listened open-mouthed. A friendship began.

"Would you be interested in meeting the Argonauts? We hold our sessions at the Bureau of Longitudes, thanks to François Barlier, one of our members, who is the Bureau's vice-president."

Even as a child, I knew that being a writer would open most doors to me.

15. Military leader famous for stating the obvious. "A quarter hour before his death, he was still alive," his troops later chanted. (Translator's note.)

16. Or at least that is what scientists thought until the early 1970s. Then life was discovered in the abyssal zones near hydrothermal springs rich in sulphur.

17. To properly gut and purge pibales, throw them into water in which tobacco leaves have steeped. Then wash them thoroughly: the skin of young fish is covered with a clinging mucus. There are now two possibilities (among others): an omelet or the frying pan. My preference is for the latter: a handful of pibales sautéd in olive oil, with

garlic and a dash of red pepper. See Jean Ferniot, "La France des terroirs gourmands," *Sélection du Reader's Digest,* Paris 1993.

18. An association links all those who believe in the potential of the sea: IOA; see website *clubdesargonautes.org*

19. Maury, *op. cit.,* pp. 50–52.

20. Those wishing to know more about these plants and their intrepid discoverers can follow my example and join the very active Scottish Rhododendron Society. Write to John Hammond at 51 Sandylane, Frestwick, Manchester M25 8RD, U.K. There also exists a Société bretonne du rhododendron, at Kerneostic Menez Rohou, 29170 Fouesnant, France.

21. Hans Leip, *Le Roman du Gulf Stream*, translated from the German by J.R. Weiland, Plon, Paris 1956. My thanks to Gérard d'Abbeville: a great seafarer, whether sailing or rowing, his knowledge of currents and their secrets is unsurpassed. It was Gérard d'Abbeville

who brought this fascinating document to my attention. [Author's note.] I have further translated this from French to English. [Translator's note.]

22. Emmanuel Le Roy Ladurie, *Histoire du climat depuis l'an mil* [a history of climate since the year 1,000], Flammarion, Paris 1967, vol. I, p. 7.

23. P. Humbert, "Documents météorologiques anciens concernant la région du mont Blanc," 1934, quoted by Emmanuel Le Roy Ladurie in *Histoire du climat depuis l'an mil, op. cit.*

24. That is, Baby Jesus. The fishermen of Peru had so named a warm current that made its appearance along their coasts at Christmas time.

25. Richard Seager, *Quarterly Journal of the Royal Meteorological Society* 128, (2002). Summary in *La Recherche*, "La Mer," special issue, February 2003.

26. Cf. *Océans et Atmosphère*, various authors,, Hachette, Paris 1966.

27. The Italian's name was Nobile; he survived and lived to a ripe old age.

28. Jacques Lacarrière, *Au coeur des mythologies: en suivant les dieux*, Gallimard, "Folio" series, Paris 2002.

29. *Anthologie sanskrite*, Payot, Paris 1947; Adapted from Louis Renou's French translation.

30. *Sailing Directions and Anchorages* of the Clyde Cruising Club, as quoted in Björn Larsson, *From Cape Wrath to Finisterre*, translated from the Swedish by Tom Geddes, Haus Publishing, "Armchair Traveller" series, London 2005, pp. 268–69.

31. *Livre des sépultures*, attributed to Guo Pu (years 276–324), quoted by Frédéric Obringer in *Feng shui, l'art d'habiter la terre*, Philippe Picquier publishers, series "Écrits dans la paume de la main," Paris 2001.

32. Ernest Eitel, *Feng shui ou principes de sciences naturelles en Chine, Annales du musée Guimet,* vol. I, 1880, quoted by Frédéric Obringer, in *Feng shui, l'art d'habiter la terre, op. cit.*, our transl.

33. See Michel Baridon, *Les Jardins*, Robert Laffont, Paris 1998.

34. "Ici Londres, les Français parlent aux Français." Opening words of Free French broadcasts from England during the German occupation of France in the 1940s. (Translator's note.)
35. Institut Français de Recherche pour l'Exploitation de la mer (translator's note).
36. Many of us are looking forward impatiently to the appearance of this book. It should be explained that Bruno Voituriez is a renowned oceanographer, formerly with Ifremer and the IRD, a specialist in the relationship between physics and biology, and moreover very well versed in matters of climate.

ATLANTIC
X
XI
XII
France
Spain
Portugal
Part of Barbary
LAKE HURON
LAKE MICHIGAN
LAKE Ontario
Lake Erie
NEW YORK
New Jersey
PENNSYLVANIA
Philadel'a
MARY LAND
Delaware Bay
VIRGINIA
OHIO RIVER
NORTH CAROLINA
SOUTH CAROLINA
GEORGIA
WEST FLORIDA
EAST FLORIDA
PART OF THE GULF of MEXICO
ATLANT